New Directions for
Child and Adolescent
Development

William Damon
EDITOR-IN-CHIEF

# Human Technogenesis: Cultural Pathways Through the Information Age

Dinesh Sharma
EDITOR

Number 105 • Fall 2004
Jossey-Bass
San Francisco

HUMAN TECHNOGENESIS: CULTURAL PATHWAYS THROUGH THE INFORMATION
AGE
*Dinesh Sharma* (ed.)
New Directions for Child and Adolescent Development, no. 105
*William Damon,* Editor-in-Chief

Microfilm copies of issues and articles are available in 16mm and 35mm,
as well as microfiche in 105mm, through University Microfilms Inc.,
300 North Zeeb Road, Ann Arbor, Michigan 48106-1346.

ISSN 1520-3247     electronic ISSN 1534-8687

NEW DIRECTIONS FOR CHILD AND ADOLESCENT DEVELOPMENT is part of The
Jossey-Bass Education Series and is published quarterly by Wiley Sub-
scription Services, Inc., a Wiley company, at Jossey-Bass, 989 Market
Street, San Francisco, California 94103-1741. Periodicals postage paid at
San Francisco, California, and at additional mailing offices. Postmaster:
Send address changes to New Directions for Child and Adolescent Devel-
opment, Jossey-Bass, 989 Market Street, San Francisco, CA 94103-1741.

*New Directions for Child and Adolescent Development* is indexed in Bio-
sciences Information Service, Current Index to Journals in Education
(ERIC), Psychological Abstracts, and Sociological Abstracts.

SUBSCRIPTIONS cost $90.00 for individuals and $205.00 for institutions,
agencies, and libraries.

EDITORIAL CORRESPONDENCE should be sent to the Editor-in-Chief, William
Damon, Stanford Center on Adolescence, Cypress Building C, Stanford
University, Stanford, CA 94305.

Jossey-Bass Web address: www.josseybass.com

# CONTENTS

# EDITOR'S NOTES

We are at the cusp of a new digitally connected world, which is giving rise to a radically different interactive culture. New questions about the process of human development are being posed as the children of this new world rapidly come of age. Recent developments in interactive information technologies pose a significant challenge to contemporary theories of life span human development, including language, socioemotional, cognitive, and personality development. How to understand the process of human development in a technologically driven sociocultural environment must be central to the study of human behavior.

The aim of the chapters that follow is to raise this challenge. They outline the rise and prevalence of the Internet and broadband technologies and their impact on theories of society and culture and then discuss some of the relevant behavioral concerns related to cultural transmission in the information age. Finally, they examine the impact of the rise of the Internet and other information technologies on cultural pathways by proposing the concept of human technogenesis as the constructive process whereby the recursive use of information technologies has an impact on the developing and the developed mind.

This volume examines how children and adults learn to use computers; children's interactive media; high-speed connectivity in the household, school, and the workplace; and the spread of interactive information technologies around the world. Academic scholarship must not remain stultified in traditional theories of child and human development while we await the next wave of technological innovations in the information industry, further accelerating the process of technological globalization.

Dinesh Sharma
Editor

DINESH SHARMA *is a senior methodologist/scientist at TNS-Global, an international market research firm based in Princeton, N.J.*

# 1

*The recent wave of innovation and adaptation to information technologies, giving rise to a new form of human technogenesis, is changing our everyday interactions in an unprecedented and paradigmatic manner, potentially reconstructing the nature and process of human development.*

# Cultural Pathways Through the Information Age

*Dinesh Sharma*

Decades of science fiction literature have imagined an interconnected universe. Communication sciences have theorized about a unified information network, giving rise to a 6-D vision (Brown and Duguid, 2000a, 2000b). The Ds in the 6-D vision stand for demassification, decentralization, denationalization, despacialization, disintermediation, and disaggregation, representing the emergence of a truly global society unleashed by information technologies. Conversely, the physical sciences have also popularized the advent of human-like machines and a new generation of robots, *Robo sapiens,* that can perform the most complex of human functions, experience human-like emotions, and cohabitate our world (Heuer, 2000a; Menzel, D'Aluisio, and Mann, 2000). Although these groundbreaking ideas are far from fully realized, they are no longer fiction or the stuff of Hollywood movies. We are indeed at the cusp of a new world that is digitally connected and peopled with robotics, if not full robots, giving rise to a radically interactive culture that is so different from the past. The children of this new world are rapidly coming of age, posing new questions about the process of human development.

The vision of a more egalitarian and global society guided the American baby boomers in the 1960s and 1970s, shaping the emergence of a computer-mediated digital world at the end of the second millennium (Tapscott, 1998). Unlike the industrial age, in this new media-saturated world, information and its exchange have become one of the sole commodities. The children of the information age are living under remarkably different human conditions compared to children of other historical epochs. As a sign of the rapidly changing times, the very young children of the baby boomers are coaching

NEW DIRECTIONS FOR CHILD AND ADOLESCENT DEVELOPMENT, no. 105, Fall 2004  © Wiley Periodicals, Inc.

their parents and grandparents about computers and digital media and on how to inhabit a world that is highly cybernated and filled with cyborgs (half humans–half machines) (Burman, 1999; Harraway, 1991). We are observing the first wave of children, families, and schools where cultural interaction is mediated through computers and other types of digital media, such as cell phones, interactive messaging, video games, digital cameras, and CD-ROMS. The computers and digital media are increasingly connected to the Internet, transcending time and space with an expanding reach and access to different lands and people. Thus, the sociocultural landscape of the digital children and their parents and educators includes a powerful new module: a computer-mediated cyberspace.

An understanding of the computer-mediated interactive environments must be central to contemporary theories of human development and psychology. Recent developments in interactive information technologies pose a significant challenge to theories of life span human development, with impacts on language, socioemotional, cognitive, and personality development. How to understand human development in a technologically driven sociocultural environment must be central to the study of human behavior that attempts to be comprehensive. This chapter addresses this challenge. It outlines an emerging area of research that will pose a significant challenge to traditional theories of child and human development. While we await the next wave of technological innovations in the information industry, further accelerating the process of technological globalization, academic scholarship must not remain stultified in traditional theories of child and human development.

## WWW: In the Beginning Was the Net

The current state of the Internet represents a culmination of developments in the history of communication. Similar to the invention of the printing press, we can barely grasp the impact of this new medium of communication:

> The Internet has revolutionized the computer and communications world like nothing before. The invention of the telegraph, telephone, radio, and computer set the stage for this unprecedented integration of capabilities. The Internet is at once a world-wide broadcasting capability, a mechanism for information dissemination, and a medium for collaboration and interaction between individuals and their computers without regard for geographic location [Leiner and others, 2000].

The history of the Internet consists of four pivotal developments that trace their roots to the cold war era (Cerf, 2000; Slevin, 2000; Zakon, 2002). First, the evolution of the Internet began in the late 1960s with research on packet switching (protocols in which messages are divided into packets before they are sent) and the federally funded Advanced Research Project Agency; this research continues to expand the information technology infrastructure along the key dimensions of scale, performance, and greater functionality. Second came the emergence of a global and complex operational infrastructure and its day-to-day management. The operational infrastructure continues to expand beyond university-led research centers to include global communication companies. Third, the social network has included a broad community of "internauts" around the globe working to create and advance the latest technology, developing the latest application, and determining how domain registry should proceed in the future. Finally, there have been commercial developments, including the transition of research findings into business deployment of an e-commerce infrastructure. The business-to-business revolution in the Internet space has taken place within the past decade, supported by the research and development in packet switching, systems and network management, and application software. While the Net may have emerged out of the American and North Atlantic Treaty Organization government intelligence necessities of the cold war era, the explosive growth of the World Wide Web has been supported globally by the post–cold war openness among commercial and research institutions.

Advancing the decline of the classical theories of society and culture, the Internet has added yet another layer of complexity to what the post-structuralists had been calling for throughout the 1990s: greater attention to the plurality of social and cultural projects and an empowerment of the peripheral voices in the age of late capitalism (Lyotard, 1984; Marcus and Fischer, 1986). The advent of the Net represents the beginning of the end of the old dichotomies about how the world is constructed in our minds and theories. We can no longer simply think of the world as parsed into two or three neat categories, such as East-West and the "Rest," developed-developing-underdeveloped, and traditional-modern-postmodern. Instead, every so-called area of darkness or backward, isolated, and exotic region of the world is potentially wired to the global information infrastructure and can participate in the major events of the world. As a flashback to ancient times, the Net has revived the archaic notions of the universe as inhabiting a global *atman* consciousness with a techno-utopian twist, where God is the ethereal cyberspace that runs on a high-speed supercomputer and broadband with infinite memory and hard drive. In more functional terms, the world of communication and printing, including the ancient Scriptures, are in the midst of a renaissance not unlike the invention of the printing press, where the printed word and the very craft of printing may be extinct in the age of electronic printing and on-line publishing.

## Are We All Logged On Now? Globalization Marches On!

The rise of the Internet has been well documented (The Standard Staff, 2000).[1] Recent studies in the United States indicate that well beyond 60 percent of households have Internet access. Locally, access to the Internet is uneven, but there is no doubt that the presence of the Internet is universal. Nielsen Net Ratings reported more than 459 million people on the Internet from home or work in twenty-seven countries during the second quarter of 2001, and these estimates have only increased since then (CommerceNet, 2001; Cyberatlas Staff, 2001; Thomas, 2001; TNS-Interactive, 2002). In many countries, home access is higher than access from work. The United States and Canada have the largest proportion of the world's Internet access: almost 41 percent of the global audience. European nations, the Middle East, and Africa consist of 27 percent of the world's Internet population, followed by Asia-Pacific (20 percent) and Latin America (4 percent).

Worldwide Internet users continue to grow. A global study by Ipsos-Reid found that the Internet has entered a new phase of development, where the developed regions have stopped growing rapidly (see Table 1.1). Western Europe (22 percent), along with the remainder of the English-speaking

## Table 1.1  Face of the Web Survey

| Region | Percentage of the Population, 2000 |
| --- | --- |
| Sweden | 65 |
| Canada | 60 |
| United States | 59 |
| Netherlands | 57 |
| Australia | 54 |
| Finland | 53 |
| Switzerland | 51 |
| Singapore | 46 |
| South Korea | 45 |
| Germany | 37 |
| Belgium | 36 |
| United Kingdom | 35 |
| Taiwan | 35 |
| Hong Kong | 34 |
| Japan | 33 |
| Urban Mexico | 33 |
| France | 30 |
| Italy | 28 |
| Urban Malaysia | 26 |
| Spain | 22 |
| Urban Brazil | 22 |
| Urban China | 21 |
| Urban Argentina | 20 |
| Poland | 19 |
| Urban Egypt | 17 |
| Urban Colombia | 17 |
| Turkey | 13 |
| Urban India | 9 |
| Urban South Africa | 6 |
| Urban Russia | 6 |

Source: Ipsos-Reid, cited in Pastore (2001a).

world (12 percent), including Australia, Canada, urban South Africa, and Britain, now constitutes a geographical region that rivals the American Internet users market. Similarly, Sweden (65 percent) and Canada (60 percent) have surpassed the United States (59 percent) with the highest proportion of Internet access in the world (Pastore, 2001a).

However, the awareness of the Internet is still not universal. At least one-fourth of the population in urban China, India, Russia, and the rest of the developing world are not aware of the Internet. In contrast, awareness of the Internet is almost universal in North America, Australia, Europe, and Japan. Without widespread home access, people in developing countries outside of urban centers have greater obstacles in using the Internet, where offices and Internet kiosks represent the main alternatives for logging on. Even in the most technologically advanced countries like the United States, about half of those without Internet access do not plan to get on-line.

The Web has begun to diversify along linguistic and cultural lines. Although still dominated by the English language and American content and cultural influences, a reflection of the modern cosmopolitan world and the American popular culture, Internet users are increasingly able to find what they need in their own language on local sites. Local cultural content has begun to play a significant role in converting less frequent users into heavy users. The Face of the Web study involved more than twenty-eight thousand interviews with on-line users in thirty countries and general consumers in thirty-five countries, conducted in early 2000, by Ipsos-Reid, the international market research firm (Ipsos-Reid, 2000).

Younger users are also growing on the Web (AOL Time Warner, 2001; Jupiter Media Metrix, 2000; Pastore, 1999), mostly in North America and the Asia Pacific region. Children under the ages of eighteen years using the Internet are projected to increase dramatically over the next five to six years. The rate of growth will be higher in the Asia-Pacific area than in North America, according to a report by Computer Economics (1999). However, there will still be more young people using the Internet in North America than in the Asia-Pacific region in 2005. The growth among the younger demographics is much slower in other parts of the world, such as Europe, Middle East, and Africa (see Table 1.2).

Not unlike the evolution of earlier media technologies (for example, television, cable TV, and direct TV), the Internet still awaits succession of technological innovations toward achieving universal penetration (McLaughlin, 2000). However, its impact is being felt in the most remote parts of the world even today. Small businesses in far-flung corners of the world are able to sell their products on-line on auction sites, reaping unimaginable profits. Individuals hungry for knowledge are able to take on-line courses on e-learning sites and buy books from on-line bookstores at their fingertips. Human rights groups are able to expose human rights violations by posting case histories on locally run political Web sites, stirring panic among governments. The march of human progress has accelerated with the invention

### Table 1.2  Internet Usage Estimates Under Eighteen Years of Age (Estimated)

|  | 2001 | 2005 |
|---|---|---|
| Africa | 90,000 | 356,700 |
| Asia Pacific | 6,209,700 | 22,230,100 |
| Europe | 6,165,200 | 15,336,500 |
| Middle East | 156,500 | 438,700 |
| North America | 13,708,800 | 36,294,400 |
| South America | 477,000 | 1,778,300 |
| Worldwide | 28,807,200 | 77,064,700 |

*Source:* Computer Economics, cited in Pastore (1999).

of the personal computer. With increasing digital convergence between Internet, cell phones, TV, and other forms of multimedia, such as digital audio and video files, it is difficult to predict what the next wave of killer applications will offer.

## "Food, Shelter, and Bandwidth" and Other Instances of Leapfrogging

One thing is clear: the dissemination of the Internet around the world will have far-reaching implications for the developing world.[2] For instance, the developing economies in the Asia-Pacific region are leapfrogging the developed world on the grounds of this new technology (Computerworld, 2001). The hi-tech mantra of the developing economies is resoundingly clear: "food, shelter, and bandwidth." Societies caught in the early phases of the demographic transition, with high levels of population growth and lower per capita income, are betting that the hi-tech sector will speed up productivity and economic growth and catapult them into positions of competitive advantage in the global economy (Keniston, 2003; Singhal and Rogers, 2001). There is an isomorphic relationship between economic development and maternal and child health or human development broadly conceived (Chen, Kleinman, and Ware, 1994; Sharma, 1998a). The new interactive technologies have already led to higher standards of living, while simultaneously avoiding some of the pitfalls of industrial development.

India, China, and Korea may account for more than 72 percent of total Internet users in the Asia-Pacific region by 2005, according to International Data Coporation (IDC) (CommerceNet, 2001; Nielsen Netratings, 2001; Pastore, 2001b). Greater China (mainland China, Hong Kong, and Taiwan) will eventually comprise nearly half of all users in this region. The business-to-business Internet commerce in the Asia-Pacific region reached 22 percent ($96.8 billion) of the worldwide total ($433.3 billion) in 2000 and 24 percent ($220 billion) in 2001. By 2005, the Asia-Pacific region will control 28 percent of the world's business-to-business Internet commerce transactions.

The Gartner Group, which produced these estimates, defines business-to-business Internet commerce as the sales of goods and services for which the order-taking process was completed over the Internet (Pastore, 2001b). A report by the Boston Consulting Group (BCG) highlights similar findings, warning Asian companies to place high priority on e-commerce, even though the initial craze over the Internet may have subsided. E-commerce is changing the basis of the business landscape around the world, and if Asian companies lag significantly behind their Western counterparts, they put their fundamental competitive advantage at risk. The BCG report was based on five hundred interviews conducted in ten countries across the region (Pastore, 2001c).

The developing countries can achieve economic growth, better standards of living, and higher levels of human development at Internet speed. India, with 3 to 4 million users, lags behind China in terms of Internet usage, according to a report by Crédit Lyonnais Securities Asia (Pastore, 2000a). The explosive growth has been driven by cheaper personal computers (PCs) and Web access through cable television. If this pace continues, the number of Internet users in India could increase as much as eleven-fold up to 30 million. Broadband access allowing faster connections by cable will be important to Internet growth in India and China because there are more televisions and cable connections in this region than PCs and regular telephone lines. Wireless use, also on an upward trend in India and China, is more cost-efficient for laying down a telecommunications infrastructure.

Thus far, I have outlined some of the macrolevel forces marking the advent of the information age all around the world. What are the implications of this revolution for cultural psychology? How are children, parents, and families adapting to these rapid changes? What is the impact of Internet technologies on the education of youngsters and adults? Are these changes significantly altering the experience of the self? These are some of the questions I examine next.

## "Shreds and Patches" in Cyberspace: Cultural Transmission in the Digital Village

Cultural interaction in the digital world is radically different in terms of time-space coordinates and day-to-day interactions (Slevin, 2000). Traditional theories of culture assume that culture as a social organization has a set of endogenous properties that are central to a group of people, which binds them together. This notion of culture is directly called into question by the free-floating and digitally mediated symbolic exchange of ideas, goods, and services.

First, the Internet opens up the public domain, making the boundaries of cultural groups more permeable. Thus, cultural practices no longer remain the domain of the elite and the few who have the resources to participate in them. Second, the recipients of cultural materials are no longer passive subjects, simply engendering the cultural influences and passing them on to the next generation. Internet has given mass access to the public forum and the ability to circulate and mediate the symbolic goods of any culture. This view may prove to be too naive about the Internet, given it is still early and the medium is completely unregulated by government agencies. Nonetheless, the rise of the Internet is having tremendous impact on the social and cultural landscape by diversifying the channels of cultural diffusion at Internet speed.

The idea of cultural diffusion has been a cornerstone of anthropological theory, the central claim of relativists against evolutionary ideas about societal and cultural progress. Proponents of cultural diffusion have long argued that the driving force behind cultural change and innovation is diffusion of tools and practices across time and place. The epochal changes in human history have occurred due to diffusion of technology and not simply because of endogenous societal forces. In essence, the central properties of any culture are more a function of historical exchange of ideas and less so of invention or discoveries of any one isolated group of people. Therefore, cultures exist in "shreds and patches," as uneven but pivotal distributions of ideas, beliefs, attitudes, and practices in a population that are highly malleable over time. This notion of culture was developed most forcefully by Robert Lowie, a student of Franz Boas (Harris, 1968), and later influenced the ideas of cultural psychologists (Shweder and LeVine, 1989). The Internet reinforces the idea of cultures as "shreds and patches" not the least due to its fast-paced technological innovativeness and ever-present access to far-flung places of the world, but, more important, due to the inventiveness it affords everyday folks in their ability to participate in cultural interactions and to be able to cause change in their environment.

The computer-mediated interactive culture has an impact on cultural transmission particularly among children and adults who are early adapters of such technologies. This has significant implications for debates within cultural psychology. How do children acquire culture? What is the role of technology in the acquisition of culture? While it is common knowledge that the level of technological development has an impact on the socio-emotional and cognitive development of children, the role of the Internet on children's acquisition of culture is relatively unexplored.

Cultural transmission is partly a function of the capacity to store information. Unlike traditional means of storing information, Internet has a huge storage capacity, with significant implications for surveillance, transmission, and control. When the wide array of digital information stored on the Internet is fully circulated, anytime and anywhere, the power of the information is truly encyclopedic. In addition, the information in cyberspace can be digitally copied and reproduced by individual users at will without any copyright concerns. This interactivity is built on an advanced information network capacity, allowing unlimited numbers of users to log on around the world. The network capacity develops into a mass medium only when skilled users are able to participate actively in changing the medium. As greater numbers of users continue to participate in the new medium in conjunction with the old media, such as television, radio, and land-line telephony, the transmission of information truly approximates a digital revolution. Such a revolution is underway all around us, not unlike the printing revolution half a millennium ago.

Channels of selective diffusion are the other key aspects of cultural transmission. The Internet offers virtually unlimited access to places around the world. A visit to a museum Web site with virtual tours of the premises and the exhibits, which invariably are free of charge, is an ideal example of cultural transmission. In a previous era, such cultural resources would have been restricted to a selective audience of a certain class and background. The suspension of normative time-space distanciation inherent in interacting with a person on-line underscores the fantastical nature of electronically mediated environments. We all assume floating identities when we are communicating by e-mail, pretending that we are totally certain that the message sent will be received at the other end. Certainly, when we visit a Web site, we take it for granted that the information is almost real and authentic. When looking at the *Mona Lisa* on-line, whether at the Web site of the Louvre or of the Museum of Modern Art in New York City, the digital representation looks almost real to the naked eye. We pretend that it is real and grounded in a time and space coordinate, while in fact it is a free-floating image. A Web page exists in a digital space held together by bits of code, but the parameters of the Web site, the Web address, the computer monitor enclosing the presentation of the Web page, and most certainly the on-line interactivity convince us that the stimulus is virtually real, articulated, and grounded.

Finally, individual privacy is the other central issue in cultural transmission, highly relevant for parents, teachers, and children. There are several new technologies that Web sites use to protect children, but none is fully safe. Filtering is perhaps the most effective and widely used method for screening content in schools and homes. The Federal Trade Commission will be charged by the U.S. Congress to enforce children's privacy on marketers and advertisers to children, outlined in the Children's Internet Protection Act. However, regulation costs may be too tough for some younger companies, which may have to shut down chatrooms or other sensitive content areas in order to comply fully with the rules.

The central issue on privacy, as Neil Postman (1994) and others have eloquently discussed in relation to television and other media channels, is the symbolic end of childhood at the behest of the market. The rise of the Internet and its increasing use by children and adults in the home mark the intensification of the commercialization of childhood. Just as every behavior has a cultural context and no behavior is culture free, there are no zones of privacy within the family that are devoid of market forces. In this age of late capitalism, the market shapes all aspects of human and collective behavior.

The uncensored use of the Internet further exemplifies this dictum, perhaps to the dismay of many child advocates and psychologists. Those child development experts who continue to believe in the innocence of childhood will be shocked to learn the nature of sensitive materials available to anyone online, ranging from pornography to hate speech. All of the cultural evidence points to the sobering realization that the pristine and idealistic view of childhood is increasingly at risk in the information age, an issue being increasingly debated by policymakers.

## E-Learning, 24/7

All U.S. public schools are now wired to the Internet, and this trend is continuing in other countries (National Center for Educational Statistics, 2001). While the student-to-computer ratio is still fairly low (approximately nine students per Internet terminal), the digitization of public schools has occurred at light speed in less than a decade. According to the report "Internet Access in US Public Schools and Classrooms: 1994–1999" by the U.S. Education Department's National Center for Educational Statistics (2000), the percentage of public schools connected to the Internet increased from 35 to 95 percent and classroom connections increased from 3 to 63 percent from 1994 to 1999. Simultaneously, the infrastructure, network connections, and their speed have also been upgraded. Although disparities exist along economic lines and among inner-city versus suburban schools, there is a significant upward trend toward universal Internet access.

A large majority of the teachers (84 percent) claim that computers and Internet access improve the quality of education, according to research by NetDay, a nonprofit technology group. Two-thirds of the teachers believe that the Internet is an important tool for research and helps meet new standards. However, just as many teachers also claim that the Internet is not fully integrated into the school routine, and only one-fourth feel compelled to use it regularly. Still, almost 80 percent of the teachers use the Internet in their classrooms, and 48 percent believe that it is essential to teaching. Nonetheless, across all demographic groups, approximately only half of them use the Internet for less than half an hour a day. The NetDay survey reached six hundred public and private school teachers across the United States by telephone during January and February 2001 (Netday, 2001; Pastore, 2001d).

Parents are always looking for more involvement, particularly using the Internet, according to a study by Learning Pays and Yankelowich Partners. A large majority of the parents (78 percent) reported that they would like to be more involved if they had greater access to teachers, curriculum, and events. Parents feel that the Web can offer the ease of access to teaching resources that would be very useful for their children. This study was conducted with a thousand interviews with randomly selected American households, where 26 percent reported having children in grades K-12 (Pastore, 2000b).

The National School Boards Foundation also reported that the significant motivation for parents (45 percent) to buy home computers and Internet access is to educate their children. The study was done with 1,735 parents of children ages two to seventeen and 601 children ages nine to seventeen. Unlike earlier findings that were critical of the Internet as stealing family time, almost 95 percent of the families reported no change or an increase in family interaction despite higher Internet use. This report also finds that schools must help narrow the digital divide because schools play a major role in providing computer and Internet access to households with less than $40,000 annual income. In such moderate- to low-income homes, 76 percent of nine to seventeen year olds connect to the Internet from school, and in similar African American homes, 80 percent log on from school (Pastore, 2000c).

Bridging the home and school gap using the Internet is one of the current trends in the area of educational technology (Heuer, 2000b). Knowledge Universe is a sizable company that operates KidsEdge.com, a collection of six Web sites: three for children and one each for parents, teachers, and grandparents. Parents, grandparents, and even teachers to some extent are able to log on to the same content topics, including childhood development, tech-talk, and family life. These sites are clearly learning spaces, not just for entertainment, providing timely assessment of how a child is doing in terms of skills and learning.

Another large conglomerate in the home-school space is the Family Education Network, supported by the Pearson Publishers, owners of Penguin and *Financial Times,* among others. It covers many bases with services such as Infoplease (on-line reference), TeacherVision (lesson plans, teacher aids, and Web site building), FunBrain (educational games), FamilyEducation (for parents), and MySchoolOnline (homework). Other key players in the home-school technology space are Kaptest, launched by the famous aptitude test preparation company; HighWired, a network of hundreds of high schools on-line; and BigChalk, which boasts a network of more than forty-three thousand middle and high schools.

A new day is dawning on learning facilitated by Internet technologies in schools, at home, and in the workplace. Table 1.3 displays potential differences in learning styles brought about by the advent of interactive learning. It may come as a surprise to those who have refrained from using computers that there is a generation of Americans who have no idea what life was like before the Internet. These youngsters are heavy consumers of all kinds of media, according to Simmons Market Research Bureau (see Table 1.4). In a study of five thousand children ages six to eleven, Simmons found that children who can go on-line consume a tremendous amount of old and new media, taking in more TV, movies, books, and magazines than those who do not. . . . These children are more likely to go to college (80 percent) compared to their off-line counterparts (72 percent). Once they arrive at college, 24 percent of them use a laptop in class,

### Table 1.3  The Interactive Shift in Learning Styles

| Classroom Learning | Interactive Learning |
|---|---|
| Linear, sequential | Nonlinear, hypermedia |
| Instruction | Construction, discovery |
| Teacher centered | Learner centered |
| School based | Lifelong |
| One-size-fits-all | Customized |

*Source:* Adapted from Tapscott (1998, p. 143).

### Table 1.4  Media Use by Kids

| Medium | On-Line Children | Off-Line Children |
|---|---|---|
| Television | 76% | 66% |
| Movies | 81 | 64 |
| Magazines | 58 | 36 |
| Books | 90 | 85 |

*Source:* Simmons Research cited in Pastore (2000c).

11 percent use a personal digital assistant, and Internet use is almost universal (Pastore 2000d).

The major source of difference in Internet adoption rates in the United States is due to economic differences, not ethnicity, according to Jupiter Communications (Pastore, 2000d). A majority of the homes with a household income of $15,000 or less may not have Internet access at home for several years to come. Families with an annual income of more than $75,000 will continue to be the biggest segment of Internet users. Although Internet use across ethnic groups varies tremendously, this gap is expected to narrow significantly by 2005. A study by Forrester Research has come to similar conclusions: regardless of ethnicity, consumers use the Internet for similar functions and to accomplish the same tasks. Within the mix of factors, such as age, education, and technology optimism, household income seems to be the key driving force for Internet access and use (Lake, 1999).

## Digital Family Networks

Due partly to the increase in women's use of computers, the Internet has emerged as a significant factor in bringing American families together, according to a study by CyberDialogue. Fifty-three percent of the respondents indicated that the Internet has brought their families together. Information seeking, educational tasks, entertainment, and leisure activities are some of the key family activities that revolve around the Internet. Eighty-four percent of the respondents claim they enjoy going on-line with their children as a joint activity. Mothers indicated they feel empowered by the Internet in planning activities for the family; the Internet not only simplifies life but is a time saver. Women see the Internet as a source of guidance and advice for children and go on-line to buy things for their family members. The study shows that the Internet has become a focal point for the American family, with its ability to strengthen communication, learning, and play. The study was conducted with 2,010 respondents in early 2001 (Pastore, 2001e).

The Internet has fostered the development of e-mail, chatrooms, instant messaging, and other popular applications that have helped bring families and communities together. Free e-mail services by major search engines such as Yahoo and MSN have fostered intrafamily communication across geographical boundaries and time zones. In metropolitan centers of developing countries today, it is equally easy to find e-mail and Internet kiosks as long-distance calling centers. The Web mail category has seen extensive growth outside both the United States and Europe. SinaMail is the most frequently used Web mail service in China and fifth worldwide, with 11.5 million mailboxes (Pastore, 2001f). Universo Online's UOLmail is Brazil's top e-mail service and ranks eighth worldwide, with 7 million users. Thirteenth in the world is RediffMail, which is widely used in India, and fourteenth is Taiwan's Kimo Mail. In addition, Hotmail and Yahoo Mail are becoming increasingly international. Another wave of indigenous Web mailers is on the way, where English is the second language. Similarly, among global Internet service providers, MSN, AOL, and Yahoo lag behind local service providers.

In a study by the Pew Trust, 62 percent of respondents like using e-mail because they can stay in touch with family members without spending money on the telephone; 72 percent of those who e-mail friends feel the same way (Pastore, 2000e). Inside digitally networked families, e-mail use is increasingly important; siblings exchange e-mail more frequently than they are inclined to call each other. Other more distant family contacts rely on e-mail more often than telephone contact. One-third of those who e-mail family members prefer e-mail communication because of the freedom to be open and frank using e-mail communication.

A long-time observer of children's use of computers cross-culturally, Seymour Papert (1996) has argued that reading and writing on the computer and Internet will replace the old print medium in the home. Instead, family interaction and learning will revolve around digitally driven media, including home entertainment centers. "I use movies and books as examples to make certain points about the computer culture because they are familiar, but in the very near future the separation of 'books,' 'movies,' and 'computers' will seem quaint and old-fashioned. Reading and writing have become so much the symbol for what is most important in children's learning that any suggestion of merging books with movies and computers evokes extremely strong feelings. But it will happen" (pp. 82–83).

## Cybercultures, Cyberselves

There are many behavioral implications of living in a computer-mediated world, particularly for children who are heavy users of this medium. Clearly, one of them is that this technology affords radically different mechanisms for the experience of the self (Wallace, 1999). First, the on-line self presentation is filled with anonymity and an air of mystery. People use code names and shorthand for describing who they are. On-line masking is very easy, and the sender can control very tightly the impressions relayed to the public. The Internet is colder than most other communication media, for it lacks a human voice and face that can reflect back. Thus, users have developed emoticons, or coded sign language, to convey emotional responses.

Yet due to these very reasons, the Internet serves as a great communication tool for complete strangers or mere acquaintances to take each other seriously, unbiased by a person's physical persona. People are more inclined to reveal openly their feelings and thoughts to the larger public when their identity is concealed. This fosters a kind of self-reflexive capacity that may not exist otherwise. This is commonly found in chatrooms, bulletin boards, and individual Web sites. People take their ideas and opinions more seriously and embellish their self-descriptions. Now, with advanced technologies, it is possible to let strangers into your homes and personal lives with digital Web cameras as if to put yourself on a stage for the world.

In a curious way, the bundling of all these technologies in cyberspace has given rise to a new dimension of the self or a cyberself. Relatively grounded in the personal and social self-structure, the cyberself is a media extension of our personality, complementing our other multiple selves. The cyberself operates in the environment of the Internet, but depending on the kind of emphasis placed on it, it may serve as an important part of the persona shown to the larger world. In this fashion, the Internet can foster an opening up of communication channels to the wider community. Anyone who puts a message on a Web site will receive a response in hours, if not minutes: someone, somewhere will be logged on and will connect.

Psychologists and other behavioral scientists are beginning to wonder about the implications of this medium for our everyday lives (Papert, 1996; Turkle, 1995; Wallace, 1999). Is the self now more open due to the virtual access it has to the larger community? What about the alienation and isolation that the Internet naturally induces due to the social and emotional coldness inherent in a computer-mediated world? The computer-mediated society may further destroy the face-to-face community in the workplace and even at home. We are inextricably tied to the digital identities we have built up on the Web, e-mail addresses, Web pages, and public information available through various social agencies. Contrary to the hopes and wishes of techno-utopians, the Internet, instead of bringing us all together, may introduce new disjunctions in the everyday presentation of the self. It is simply too early to intuit where this technology will lead us in the formation of a new kind of social and cultural order. However, it is undisputed that this new form of connectivity is fundamentally reshaping our lives.

## Human Technogenesis

We are living in a rapidly changing world. The march of human progress and development, from nomadic hunters and gatherers to sedentary agrarians to industrialists, has brought us to what is now widely known as the information age. The opening scene of the movie *2001: A Space Odyssey* is a fitting image for the conclusion of this chapter: a prehistoric *Homo sapiens* trying to devise something with the tools at his disposal flings an ancestral bone into the air, which fades into the image of a spaceship floating in intergalactic space with advanced humans at the helm. It is only fitting that as a highly evolved symbol-making primate, humans will discover new principles about the universe with their capacity to manipulate symbolic tools. Binary numbers, computers, and the Internet. *Homo informaticus!*

The successive transmission of the tools over time has ensured the survival and progress of the human species (Harris, 1968; Kuper, 1994). We have come full circle from nomadic hunters-and-gatherers to virtual nomads in the information age. Now that the human search for subsistence and well-being is ever expanding and leading to greater longevity and human survival, we have become nomads in the technological and media-saturated world of our own creation. We work not only on matter but on machines; we are mediators of symbolic content and thus replaceable by smart machines. We travel at a much faster pace than we ever thought humanly possible, living in multiple time zones simultaneously. We uproot more often than ever before in search of better standards of living and live in several homes in a lifetime, often across geographical and cultural boundaries. We have access to the farthest corners of the world at our fingertips from anywhere in the world, yet we are bound by social class, ethnicity, and national boundaries. We can relate to people of diverse backgrounds if we speak a common language and work on shared tasks, but our lives are determined by the conditions of our birth, the ontogenetic pathways we create out of the bricks and mortars of our early experiences. Our global identifications are the most recent layers of our social and cultural heritage, built on millions of years of phylogenetic evolution. Although we have more information and better tools for information gathering at our disposal, we are restlessly searching for better ways to build a more unified world.

According to technofuturists (Clark, 2000; Toffler, 1991), one way forward is through better technology and faster means of communication. As evident from the data and observations presented in this chapter, the advent of the computer and the Internet has given rise to what I believe is a new form of human-technology nexus, human technogenesis.[3] Human technogenesis is the process by which humans construct, manipulate, and interact

Figure 1.1.  Human Technogenesis in Relation to Ontogenesis
and Phylogenesis

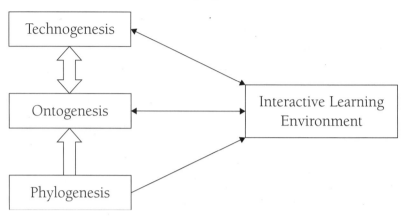

with information technologies, resulting in the sociocultural process of interactive development that continually reshapes our representations and experiences of the world. The everyday interaction with computer-mediated technologies leads to the acquisition of new functions and structures of the mind and to a new social and cultural formation about how we think the everyday world is organized (see Figure 1.1). The evidence is all around us, especially in the digitally hand-held devices that we use to organize our lives, the cell phones we use to communicate with each other, and the ease with which we are able to virtually travel to distant places. The interactive nature of human technogenesis is reshaping our individual and collective mind in an unprecedented manner with its impact on human perceptions, emotions, and cognitions with everyday use of interactive devices. Human technogenesis represents the convergence of human mind and its activities as mediated through computers or Internet technologies, made possible by the recent intensification of personal computers and the Internet in our everyday lives. Although the advent of computer-mediated technologies and the Internet is at an early stage of development, it has had a profound impact on our sense of who we are as individuals and collective beings such that we cannot imagine a world devoid of such technologies.

## Cultural Pathways Through the Information Age

In a series of writings (Sharma, 1996, 1997, 1998a, 1998b, 2000a, 2000b, 2003; Sharma and Fischer, 1998), I have proposed an original framework for human development across cultures, arguing for the multiplicity of cultural contexts and the ontogenetic complexity of cultural pathways. Encouraged by the new developments in the field of culture and cognition, against the positivistic and mechanistic views of psychology, I have drawn implications for the study of social emotions across cultures. I have refrained from making broad generalizations about the process of human development in other domains. However, the central claim put forth in my previous publications is valid for other domains of human development, particularly cognitive development.

Cultural research on populations around the world needs to focus on the nature and process of developmental change in cultural contexts. Populations around the world have been represented as static subjects of history and social science for a very long time, stretching back to the origins of the science of culture and society. For example, studies within cultural psychology and cross-cultural research have been focused on domain-specific microprocesses, such as language, cognition, emotions, and personality attributes, but not on the dynamics of developmental change in human lives across cultures. Eschewing studies of developmental change has meant avoiding generalizations about the interplay between culture and personality. I have traced the roots of this impasse to certain epistemological positions within the history of culture and personality studies and its later reincarnations, such as psychological anthropology and cultural psychology. Within the context of cognitive development, it remains the case that the study of cognition across cultures has not systematically mapped the cultural pathways of human cognition across different populations around the world.

Examining the nature of Internet technologies and its impact on human technogenesis underscores the need for dynamic models of cognitive development that take into consideration the interactivity between computer and Internet use and the human mind. The research on cognitive development across cultures has remained closely tied to ideas about contextual theory and situated cognition (Lave and Wenger, 1991; Rogoff, 1991; Segall, Dasen, Berry, and Poortinga, 1990; Shweder and LeVine, 1989). With the rise of information technologies and the intensification of hypertechnologies around the world, the study of cognitive development cannot remain stultified in static representations of the social and cultural world. The nature of interactivity inherent in computer-mediated communications should encourage researchers studying cognitive development in positive ways toward studies of information technology and its impact on human development. Figure 1.1 outlines the role of human technogenesis in shaping the ontogenetic developmental pathways, giving rise to new forms of adaptive behavior within the evolutionary context. I believe technogenetic psychology, or the study of the interaction between computer-mediated technologies and the human mind within a cultural context, represents the cutting edge of research on human development. Computer-mediated technologies are one of the main engines for globalization around the world. Therefore, the process of human technogenesis potentially influences all spheres of individual, social, and cultural life, an issue fully explored in this volume.

The following chapters examine the process of human technogenesis from several important angles. Chapter Two by John Carey explores the role of broadband communication on expressive communication in home, school, and the workplace. Unlike narrowband, which has a limited range of transmission, broadband can display verbal and nonverbal communication in rich contextual displays of face-face interactions and can elevate everyday human interaction across time and space. The role of broadband technology across cultures has remained at the level of policy discussions. However, it has great potential for advancing communication within and across cultures and for advancing children's learning and human communication within all kinds of organizations.

Chapter Three, by Zheng Yan and Kurt Fischer, outlines the cultural pathways through the information age by examining how children and adults learn to use computers. This chapter exemplifies the kind of empirical research that is needed to fully grasp the impact of interactive technologies on human development, while highlighting the need for path-breaking cross-cultural research in the field. The developmental challenges of the information age are inherently cross-cultural in nature as the new interactive technologies foster connectivity and cultural fusion.

Chapter Four, by Angel Gordo Lopéz and Erica Burman, examines the impact of the new information technologies on the social reconstruction of children and childhood. The authors reach the profound conclusion that the new technologies infuse children and childhood with emotional capital of the new information economy, while simultaneously blurring the distinctions between biology and technology, as represented by the characters of *Teletubbies,* the well-known children's program. They alert us that we must be attuned to this new, subtler layer of discourse about childhood if we are to participate fully in the everyday lives of the next generation of children and young adults.

## Notes

1. I rely on market research reports, compiled by various well-known marketing research companies, to present a demographic and geographical profile of the Internet. When culture-specific data are available, I use them as well. In other instances, I use global statistics on U.S. Internet usage. The data presented in Table 1.1 represent conservative estimates, in order to be cautious about the growth of the Internet, that have now been well surpassed by current trends.

2. I rely on reports that use a variety of econometric techniques to project future economic trends. Again, I use culture-specific data when they are available.

3. The term *technogenesis* is borrowed from geological sciences, where it refers to the changes in the sedimentation of the earth's sphere and the environment due to the introduction of technological changes; for instance, the construction of a hydraulic dam changes the water flow, river beds, and irrigation of agricultural land. The adverse impact of a nuclear plant on the geophysical space that surrounds it is another example of catastrophic technogenesis. Human technogenesis, as used here, refers to the role of human perception, emotions, and cognition in the interplay of human mind and interactive information technologies. The use of interactive technologies over a long period of time

potentially affects not only our habits and lifestyles but also our everyday perceptions of the world. This use of the term is closer to the meaning of the term *technogenesis* as presented in the recent science fiction written by Syne Mitchel, and may have similarities with the way this term is used by the Stevens Institute of Technology to describe its educational curriculum. However, the latter use refers to infrastructural change and the former to individual change.

# References

AOL TimeWarner. "Digital East Meets Digital West." [http://www.aoltimewarner.com/globalview/legend.html]. 2001.

Brown, J. S., and Duguid, P. *The Social Life of Information.* Boston: Harvard Business School Press, 2000a.

Brown, J. S., and Duguid, P. "Ideas to Feed Your Business: Re-Engineering the Future." [http://www.thestandard.com/article/0,1902,14013,00.html]. 2000b.

Burman, E. "The Child and the Cyborg." In A. J. Gordo-López and I. Parker (eds.), *Cyberpsychology.* New York: Routledge, 1999.

Cerf, V. "Brief History of Internet." [http://www.isoc.org/history/brief.shtml]. 2000.

Chen, L., Kleinman, A., and Ware, N. *Health and Social Change in International Perspective.* Boston: Harvard School of Public Health, 1994.

Clark, A. C. *2001: A Space Odyssey.* New York: Mass Market Paperback, 2000.

CommerceNet. "Estimating the Worldwide Internet Population." [http://www.commerce.net/research/stats/wwstats.html#asiapacific]. 2001.

Computer Economics. "Western Hemisphere Internet Users Under Age 18–2003 to 2007." [http://www.computereconomics.com/page.cfm?name=Internet%20Demographics%20%26%20Trends]. 1999.

Computerworld. "Asia-Pacific's Satellite Broadband Market Is Set to Fly." [http://www.thestandard.com/article/0,1902,27739,00.html]. 2001.

Cyberatlas Staff. "Worldwide Adoptions of Internet Continues to Increase." [http://www.cyberatlas.com/big_picture/geographics/article/0,,5911_875361,00.html]. 2001.

Harraway, D. *Simians, Cyborgs, and Women.* London: Verso, 1991.

Harris, M. *The Rise of Anthropological Theory.* New York: Crowell, 1968.

Heuer, S. "Daydreamers." [http://www.thestandard.com/article/0,1902,12457,00.html]. 2000a.

Heuer, S. "Putting the Home in Homework." [http://www.thestandard.com/article/0,1902,18236,00.html]. 2000b.

Ipsos-Reid. "The Face of the Web Survey." [http://www.ipsos-na.com/news/pressrelease.cfm?id=2024]. 2000.

Jupiter Media Metrix. "Income and Age, Not Ethnicity, to Remain Largest Gap for US Digital Divide." [http://www.jmm.com/xp/jmm/press/2000/pr_061500a.xml]. 2000.

Keniston, K. "Can the Cultures of India Survive the Information Age?" In R. Narasimha, J. Sinivasan, and S. K. Biswas (eds.), *The Dynamics of Technology.* Thousand Oaks, Calif.: Sage, 2003.

Kuper, A. *The Chosen Primate: Human Nature and Cultural Diversity.* Cambridge, Mass.: Harvard University Press, 1994.

Lake, D. "Net Use Divided Between 'Haves' and 'Have Nots.'" [http://www.thestandard.com/article/0,1902,5486,00.html]. 1999.

Lave, J., and Wenger, D. *Situated Learning.* Cambridge: Cambridge University Press, 1991.

Leiner, B., and others. "A Brief History of the Internet." [http://www.isoc.org/internet/history]. 2000.

Lyotard, J. F. *The Postmodern Condition: A Report on Knowledge.* Minneapolis: University of Minnesota Press, 1984.

Marcus, G. E., and Fischer, M. J. (1986). *Anthropology as Cultural Critique: An Experimental Moment in the Human Sciences.* Chicago: University of Chicago Press.

McLaughlin, J. "Planet Web: Equalizer or Divider?" [http://www.thestandard.com/article/0,1902,20321.00.html]. 2000.

Menzel, P., D'Aluisio, F., and Mann, C. *Robo-Sapiens: Evolution of a New Species.* Cambridge, Mass.: MIT Press, 2000.

National Center for Educational Statistics. "Percent of Public Schools with Internet Access, Percent of Instructional Rooms with Internet Access in Public Schools, and Ratio of Students per Instructional Computer with Internet Access, by School Characteristics: Selected Years 1994 to 1999." [http://nces.ed.gov/quicktables]. 2001.

Netday. The Internet, Technology and Teachers. [http://www.netday.org/anniversary_survey.htm]. 2001.

Nielsen Netratings. "Internet Penetration Leap-Frogging Telephone Access in Developing Countries." [http://asiapacific.acnielsen.com.au/news.asp?newsID=50]. 2001.

Papert, S. *The Connected Family: Bridging the Digital Generation Gap.* Atlanta, Ga.: Longstreet Press, 1996.

Pastore, M. "Number of Kids On-line Is Growing." [http://www.cyberatlas.com/big_picture/demographics/article/0,,5901_150161,00.html]. 1999.

Pastore, M. "India May Threaten China as King of Netizens." [http://www.cyberatlas.com/big_picture/geographics/article/0,,5911_309751,00.html]. 2000a.

Pastore, M. "Parents See Net as an Educational Aid." [http://www.cyberatlas.com/markets/education/article/0,,5951_328051,00.html]. 2000b.

Pastore, M. "Online Kids Consume More Media." [http://www.cyberatlas.com/big_picture/demographics/article/0,,5901_425501,00.html]. 2000c.

Pastore, M. "Digital Divide More Economic Than Ethnic." [http://www.cyberatlas.com/big_picture/demographics/article/0,,5901_395581,00.html]. 2000d.

Pastore, M. "Women Use the Web to Change the Social Landscape." [http://www.cyberatlas.com/big_picture/demographics/article/0,,5901_361241,00.html]. 2000e.

Pastore, M. "U.S. Share of Internet Users Continue to Shrink, Hypergrowth Over." [http://www.cyberatlas.com/big_picture/geographics/article/0,,5911_769451,00.html]. 2001a.

Pastore, M. "Internet Users in Asia-Pacific to Surpass U.S. Users in 2005." [http://www.cyberatlas.com/big_picture/geographics/article/0,,5911_767371,00.html]. 2001b.

Pastore, M. "Online B-to-B Markets in Asia-Pacific." [http://www.cyberatlas.com/big_picture/demographics/article/0,,5901_425501,00.html]. 2001c.

Pastore, M. [http://cyberatlas.internet.com/markets/education/print/0,,5951734761,00.html]. 2001d.

Pastore, M. "Mom Using Web to Bring Families Together." [http://www.cyberatlas.com/big_picture/demographics/article/0,,5901_705131,00.html]. 2001e.

Pastore, M. "Email Goes International in 2000." [http://www.cyberatlas.com/big_picture/applications/article/0,,1301_710381,00.html]. 2001f.

Postman, N. *The Disappearance of Childhood.* New York: Vintage Books, 1994.

Rogoff, B. *Apprenticeship in Thinking.* New York: Oxford University Press, 1991.

Segall, M. H., Dasen, P. R., Berry, J. W., and Poortinga, Y. *Human Behavior in Global Perspective.* New York: Pergamon Press, 1990.

Sharma, D. "Childcare, Family and Culture: Lessons from India." Unpublished doctoral dissertation, Harvard University, 1996.

Sharma, D. "Cultural Pathways to Early Socioemotional Development." In *Proceedings from the Society for Research on Child Development Biennial Meeting.* Washington, D.C. Ann Arbor, MI: SRCD Publications, 1997a.

Sharma, D. "Children's Social and Cultural Worlds: The Rural-Urban Transition." In K. Ekberg (ed.), *Urban Childhood. Proceedings from the International, Interdisciplinary*

*Conference, Norwegian Center for Child Research, Trondheim, Norway.* Trondhiem, Norway: Norwegian Center for Child Research, 1997b.

Sharma, D. *Culture and Childhood Risks: A Population Perspective.* Educational Resources Information Center, Elementary and Early Childhood Education. (ED395671) [http://www.ericfacility.net/teams/Search.do?action=102]. 1998a.

Sharma, D. "Discursive Voice of Psychoanalysis: A Case for Culturally Constituted Defenses." *Culture and Psychology,* 1998b, *4*(1), 49–64.

Sharma, D. "Children's Sociocultural and Familial Worlds: Pathways and Risks Through the Demographic Transition Theory." In A. L. Comunian and U. P. Gielen (eds.), *International Perspectives on Human Development* (pp. 195–210). Lengerich, Germany: Pabst, 2000a.

Sharma, D. "Infancy and Childhood in India: A Critical Review." *International Journal of Group Tensions,* 2000b, *29*(3/4), 219–251.

Sharma, D. *Childhood, Family and Sociocultural Change in India.* New York: Oxford University Press, 2003.

Sharma, D., and Fischer, K. "Socioemotional Development Across Cultures: Context, Complexity and Pathways." In D. Sharma and K. Fischer (eds.), *Socioemotional Development Across Cultures.* New Directions for Child and Adolescent Development, no. 81. San Francisco: Jossey-Bass, 1998.

Sharma, D., and LeVine, R. A. "Cultures of Childhood: Interdisciplinary Perspectives on Socio-Emotional Development of Infants and Young Children." In *Proceedings from the Growing Mind,* Jean Piaget Centennial Conference, University of Geneva, Switzerland, 1996.

Sharma, D., and LeVine, R. A. "Childcare in India: A Comparative View of Infant Social Environments." In D. Sharma and K. Fischer (eds.), *Socioemotional Development Across Cultures.* New Directions for Child and Adolescent Development, no. 81. San Francisco: Jossey-Bass, 1998.

Shweder, R., and LeVine, R. A. *Culture Theory: Essays on Mind, Self and Emotions.* Cambridge: Cambridge University Press, 1989.

Singhal, A., and Rogers, E. M. *India's Communication Revolution.* Thousand Oaks, Calif.: Sage, 2001.

Slevin, J. *The Internet and Society.* London: Polity Press, 2000.

Standard Staff. "It's an e-World After All." [http://www.thestandard.com/article/0,192,12555,00.html]. 2000.

Tapscott, D. *Growing Up Digital: The Rise of the Net Generation.* New York: McGraw Hill, 1998.

Thomas, B. "Global Internet Trends: North America Losing Dominance." [http://www.ciol.com/content/news/trends/101122703.asp]. 2001.

TNS-Interactive. "Global eCommerce Report 2002." [http://www.tns-i.com/press/release/ger2002.htm].

Toffler, A. *The Third Wave.* New York: Bantam Books, 1991.

Turkle, S. *Life on Screen: Identity in the Age of the Internet.* New York: Weinfeld and Nicolson, 1995.

Wallace, P. *The Psychology of the Internet.* Cambridge: Cambridge University Press, 1999.

Zakon, H. "Hobbes' Internet Timeline, Version 7." [http://www.zakon.org/robert/internet/timeline/]. 2002.

*DINESH SHARMA is a senior methodologist/scientist at TNS-Global, an international market research firm based in Princeton, N.J.*

# 2

*An understanding of the structure and functions of expressive communication in face-to-face communication and audiovisual media can inform the development of new educational services for human development across cultures in the emerging broadband environment.*

# Expressive Communication and Human Development in the New Broadband Environment

*John Carey*

In assessing potential uses for the new broadband environment that is replacing older narrowband networks such as dial-up Internet service providers, much effort has been focused on business applications, such as entertainment, corporate training, video business meetings, and very-high-capacity wireless local area networks for business users (Noam, Groebel, and Gerbarg, 2002). At the same time, there is an important human development dimension that has received little attention: expressive communication. Expressive communication refers to gestures, tone of voice, body orientation, and other nonverbal signals that are present in face-to-face settings, as well as music, sound effects, color, motion video, animated graphics, and other affective signals that are present in audiovisual media such as films and videotapes.

Expressive communication is important because it is a vital component in human communication. In face-to-face contexts, it builds and maintains relationships among people, communicates emotion, and helps us to understand the meanings that are conveyed through words (Kendon, 1989). In designed media such as films or videotapes, expressive communication serves to grab and hold our attention, delight and entertain us, and modify or reinforce the meanings conveyed through words, graphics, and pictures. Expressive communication is also important in human development because it provides richness to the communication exchange among parents, children, and teachers. It enhances social interaction and learning by adding a dimension of understanding that goes beyond simple words and facts. This dimension in human interaction has been restricted in narrowband environments such as dial-up Web access but could flourish in broadband multimedia environments.

In order for expressive communication to flourish in the new broadband environment, it has to gain the attention of those who plan and design applications. Furthermore, planners need at least some understanding of the structure and functions of expressive communication in order to enhance this form of communication in new educational applications. For example, designing a system to enhance expressive communications may have an impact on screen size and resolution, the number of screens or channels used, and audio fidelity, among other system characteristics.

It will not be easy to bring attention to expressive communication or to develop an understanding of its functions and importance. Expressive communication tends to be beneath the surface of our consciousness. It has been described as a language that is written nowhere, understood by a few, and yet used and responded to by everyone (Birdwhistell, 1969). At the same time, there are many commonplace illustrations that can raise awareness about expressive communication and point to some of its functions as well as its importance. For example, are the qualities of a master teacher in an educational setting likely to come through in a written transcript of that teacher's spoken words? What would an observer need to see, hear, or feel in order for these qualities to come through? Could a person learn how to ride a bicycle, dance, or perform surgery based solely on a written description? Similarly, the power and functions of these expressive components in designed multimedia such as a movie can be demonstrated by turning off the sound and watching the movie as a series of still frames.

Research about the emotional and social relationships between people and technology is not new. Reeves and Nass (1996) demonstrated that people often treat technologies such as computers and television like real people and even attribute personality traits to computers. Turkle (1992) has explored the way bonds are formed among people using technology to communicate. Johnson (1997) has shown that computer experience flows back to the everyday world and influences how people perceive face-to-face reality. Much of the existing body of literature is based on studies of text-based computer-mediated communication (Soukup, 2000). It shows the importance of expressive communication in narrowband environments but also the limited ways available to express this form of communication. For example, many people use emoticons, or coded sign language, such as ":)" to add expressive meaning to e-mail. However, tone of voice and facial expressions provide a richer palette to communicate expressive meanings. Research about virtual reality systems has also touched on these issues. Unfortunately, much useful research about expressive communication in virtual reality systems has been obscured by the hyperbole of futurists and virtual reality proponents (Rheingold, 1991).

There is an important cross-cultural dimension as well. In the past, many new telecommunication technologies and content for them were developed in the United States, adopted first by Americans, and distributed later to other countries. Some criticized this process as a form of cultural media imperialism, especially as it has related to television programming (Cairncross, 1997). However, this has not been the case with broadband. At the end of 2003, the United States ranked eleventh in broadband penetration (Hopkins, 2004). Three of the top four countries with the highest rate of broadband penetration are in Asia; five European nations also led the United States. In addition, many of the social and psychological patterns associated with the use of advanced technologies have begun outside the United States and then migrated to America, for example, the use of advanced cell phones as a form of personal expression and to foster interpersonal networks by young female Japanese (Forlano, 2003).

This chapter discusses some general issues associated with expressive communication, reviews specific functional and structural issues associated with person-to-person communication over a broadband network and person-to-machine interactions that take place using broadband multimedia, presents an agenda of research questions, and draws a few conclusions about how expressive communication can enhance learning and human development.

## Expressive Communication

What are the basic characteristics of expressive communications? How are these signals structured, and what functions do they serve? Furthermore, what are the implications of these characteristics for emerging broadband multimedia environments and human development?

**Structural Characteristics.**  One important structural characteristic of most expressive communications is that they are analogic. That is, just as an engineer can distinguish between two broad types of signal (analog and digital) in a telecommunications context, it is possible to group human communications into two broad classes: analog and digital. Analog human communications are in some way like the thing they represent. So a gesture may be large and expansive when a person is talking about a large object, or the pitch of a person's voice may rise as he becomes angry or excited. By contrast, digital human communications are an arbitrary representation of meaning. For example, most words are digital human communications. They do not generally share any characteristics of the objects or actions they represent; the word *tree* shares no characteristics with an actual tree.

Analog human communications include gestures, tone of voice, facial movements, touch, skin tones, body orientation, and spatial relationships between individuals who are interacting. Digital human communications consist primarily of words and numbers. In general, we use analog human communications to convey emotions, messages about relationships, and other affective meanings, and we use digital human communications to convey analytical and more precise messages. Both are essential in human development. It is interesting and important to note that as our technological environment moves from analog to digital and network bandwidth increases, we are greatly expanding our capacity to transmit analog human communications. For example, a dial-up Web connection cannot show accurately the motion in the gesture of a teacher or the facial movements of children responding to what they are trying to learn.

It is also important to note that expressive communication is a component in a multichannel human communication system. Gestures, facial expressions, and other analog human communications as well as digital communications such as words and numbers are all components in an integrated multichannel system of face-to-face interaction. The technological limitations of previous generations of media have fostered single-channel communications in which analog and digital components were isolated from each other; examples are a book, a telephone call, and a phonograph record. In the emerging broadband environment, there is an opportunity to reintegrate the multichannel signals that have been isolated in many earlier media.

The temporal component of many expressive communications is another noteworthy structural characteristic. That is, many expressive communications, such as facial movements, exist in time and lose much of their meaning when captured in a discontinuous medium such as a still photograph. Until recently, the Web was limited to still photographs and static graphics. The new broadband environment presents an opportunity to restore temporal features such as movement to communication exchanges between people in a range of settings as well as in designed media.

In addition, most expressive communications become meaningful to us only when we understand the context in which they occur. Our interpretation of a gesture may change if we know that a person making the gesture is alone or with a group, in a casual setting or a formal one, sitting close to another person or several feet away from that person. Here as well, many of the media that were available in the past limited the amount of contextual information that could be transmitted. For example, if someone transmitted a wide shot of a group in a classroom, providing contextual information, details of facial expression were lost. If someone transmitted a close-up shot, details about the setting or context were lost. In some of the new broadband environments, it is possible to transmit both contextual information and facial details at the same time and give the viewer an opportunity to scan a scene the way our eyes scan a scene in everyday life.

**Functional Characteristics.** Expressive communications often convey information about relations and emotions. They are more affective than analytical. In addition, they often communicate multiple messages. For example, a person's facial expression may communicate that he feels confident about what he is saying, likes the people he is talking to, and did not sleep well the previous night. In human development, it is important to develop the skill of interpreting simultaneous, multiple meanings that are the fabric of social interactions. It is critical for a student to know that a teacher is engaged in a topic, uncertain about a conclusion, tired, and trying to communicate that the point under discussion is very important. All of these meanings may be conveyed simultaneously. A student must learn how to grasp these simultaneous multiple messages, sort them out, and make use of the relevant content in learning a lesson and developing a relationship with a teacher.

Expressive communications also serve an important redundancy role in relation to words. They can reinforce the message conveyed by words and reduce the chance of error in interpreting what someone says. They can modify or even change the meaning conveyed by words, as in a wink that accompanies a sentence and indicates that the speaker's words should not be interpreted literally. Here too it is critical in human development to process and comprehend "messages about messages" that tell us what is ironic, humorous, or facetious.

At a fundamental level, expressive communications often tell us about the rules or codes that should be applied when interpreting a message. As Bateson (1968) observed, a "distortion of messages occurs when the persons involved differ from each other in their rules or assumptions governing the making and understanding of messages—their explicit and implicit rules of coding" (p. 19). We need to communicate about the rules we are using in sending and receiving information. Much of this meta-communication is in the expressive channel.

The structure and functions of expressive communication in two-way human communication are paralleled in many ways by expressive communication in designed media. Color provides a useful example. Arnheim (1971) assessed the functions of color in designed media and noted that "the experience of color resembles that of affect or emotion" (p. 324). He observed further that color serves multiple functions; for example, it identifies objects and happenings, conveys moods, represents ideas, concentrates attention, and serves as a counterpoint to the meaning conveyed by another visual form. While it may be beneficial to explore these parallel functions in greater depth, it is more productive to separate the two major forms of expressive communication, that is, person-to-person communication and media productions, and explore some of the design issues and research questions raised by each.

## Person-to-Person Communication in New Broadband Environments

How can we apply our knowledge about expressive communication in face-to-face settings to person-to-person communication in the new broadband environment? Furthermore, how can we use the new environment to overcome the limitations of earlier narrowband media and support more effective learning, as well as general human development? A few key issues can help to illuminate a general approach to accomplishing these tasks.

**Interactional Synchrony.** In face-to-face settings, people are in a synchronous relationship with each other; they coexist in time. Furthermore, people who interact are generally in a synchronous relationship whereby the movements and speech patterns of one person are rhythmically coordinated with those of the person or persons with whom they are interacting. This interactional synchrony serves many functions. It helps people to manage who will speak next (turn taking), provides subtle messages of agreement or disagreement, and, most important, helps to create a state of communication that allows information and meaning to flow easily.

The absence of interactional synchrony can disrupt the easy flow of information. Many people have experienced the subtle disruption caused by satellite transmission of a telephone call that delays responses by mere milliseconds. A small delay in receiving the signal makes it difficult to interrupt or respond at appropriate times. The two speakers are out of sync. Another example is provided by narrow bandwidth video teleconferencing systems that sometimes lack a synchronous relationship between voice and picture. In response to such disruptions in synchrony, many people switch to a different mode of interacting—one that is more like earlier switched radio transmissions in which one person speaks at a time and there is no overlap or quick interruptions. The new broadband environment will provide an opportunity to restore synchrony between voice and body movement of each speaker, as well as interactional synchrony among two or more speakers.

**Feedback.** Feedback is a critically important dimension in face-to-face settings. As Bateson (1968) observed, "For every human being there is an edge of uncertainty about what sort of message he is emitting, and we all need, in the final analysis, to see how our messages are received in order to discover what they were" (p. 18). Feedback for a teacher includes student eyes that are alive or glazed over. Feedback for a person on a telephone call is the minimal "uh-huh" signaling that the other party is still listening, follows or does not follow a given point, and agrees or disagrees.

Feedback has been limited in many telecommunication systems. Frequently, there is no visual feedback at all, as in audio teleconferencing. Even audio feedback may be restricted or cut off in some systems. One example that many have experienced is an audio teleconference in which the audio is controlled by manual switches. Here, a speaker must talk to others on the teleconference with no audio feedback—no "uh-huhs," not even a cough. This can be very disconcerting for a teacher who uses such a system for distance learning. Similarly, one-way television transmissions such as live video telecourses often lack even audio feedback. It is difficult for ordinary people (those with no training in acting or performing before a camera) to speak into a camera knowing that a live audience can see and hear the presentation while receiving no feedback about their reactions. Here too new broadband environments offer an opportunity to provide not just minimal feedback but a rich stream of feedback mechanisms.

**Social Context.** The social context in which a communication occurs adds information to the human communication stream and helps those receiving information to interpret its meaning. Social context includes physical information such as what people are wearing and what type of room they are in, as well as customs or norms of behavior in a given setting, the backgrounds of those participating in the exchange, and the reasons that a meeting, class, or discussion was formed. In narrow channel environments, elements of social context may be eliminated, restricted, or translated into a form that can be communicated over the channel; for example, a person can describe the room where she is sitting for listeners who cannot see it. In broadband environments, more elements of the social context can be communicated, and there is less need to translate these elements into another mode such as verbal description. Furthermore, listeners or viewers in some cases may be able to exercise control over what they see and hear, for example, panning a camera at a distant site or manipulating images in a video windows environment to show a face full screen or in a corner of the video window.

**Stereo for Spatial Information and Greater Dynamic Range of Expressive Features.** Hearing with two ears instead of one serves important functions in face-to-face settings. It helps us to locate speakers in space and filter the sounds we want to hear from a background din of many conversations and environmental noise. In earlier person-to-person media, such as audio and video telelearning, there was little use of stereo to help listeners locate speakers or to help filter information. Similarly, the low dynamic range and frequency response of many teleconferencing systems compresses the range of expressive features such as pitch and volume. Furthermore, the low video scanning rate of many teleconferencing systems discouraged people from using rapid or broad gestures; such gestures often created a disruption of the visual image on the monitor. The new broadband environment can provide stereo sound for spatial information as well as higher-fidelity sound and faster scanning rates that will support a greater dynamic range in expressive features such as volume, pitch, and gestures.

**Expressive Communication and Screen Resolution.** The new broadband environment includes not only higher-speed transmission of Web services but also greater bandwidth and more efficient signal compression in cable, satellite, and over-the-air video transmissions. One use for this broadband environment is high-definition television (HDTV). HDTV has many advantages, including one that has received relatively little attention: it displays skin tones and minor facial movements that are not readily captured on older television systems, even during a close-up shot. Minor changes in skin coloration can signal anger, excitement, and other emotions. Minor facial movements convey a wide range of information and often provide clues concerning how a speaker feels about what he or she is saying.

**Large Screens, Wide Screens, and Video Window Environments.** In face-to-face settings, our eyes can observe a large visual area (or pan across it) and then focus narrowly on a smaller area, such as a person's face or a finger that is tapping nervously. In mediated situations, the camera is a surrogate for our eyes—panning and zooming—although it functions in a manner that is different from our eyes and brain. However, we do not generally control the camera, so we cannot manipulate it as we do our eyes in a face-to-face setting.

In the future, large and wide screens with high resolution will offer an opportunity for our eyes to function as they do in face-to-face settings. That is, the screen will be able to display a large, high-resolution panorama, and each participant will be able to focus on large or small areas within the screen. Furthermore, in a video windows environment, it may be possible to employ different resolutions for different visual elements on the screen; for example, the face of a speaker might be in one window with a very high resolution while the background screen might show other participants at a lower resolution. Much of the work in this area has been for virtual reality systems used in manufacturing, medicine, and video games, but some work has addressed education and human development (Biocca, 1992).

## Person-to-Machine Interactions in Multimedia Environments

Person-to-machine interactions in the new broadband environment are distinguished from person-to-person communications in that the former typically involves interaction by a person with designed content, while the latter typically involves interaction between one person or a group and another person or group. The design of content and user interfaces for person-to-machine multimedia raises a number of interesting questions.

Expressive communication in person-to-machine multimedia may be conveyed through motion video, music, animated graphics, sound effects, and other system features. These can be very powerful tools for communicating or evoking affective content such as suspense, delight, tension, and humor. Indeed, they are core elements or building blocks for creating entertainment and aesthetic experiences with these media. What are the characteristics of these building blocks, and how can they be enhanced in the new broadband environment? A few characteristics and issues associated with enhancing expressive communication in multimedia environments are outlined below.

**Time and Space.** Motion video can render the experience of time and space in everyday life as well as manipulate time and space. Both have many applications. Since all behavior takes place in a time and space continuum, it is very important to be able to render these qualities in recorded media. In training, teaching, and other applications, motion video can demonstrate how things work, move, and change. This in turn can give viewers a feeling about things, as well as an analytical understanding of them.

The manipulation of time and space—through editing, slow motion, speeded-up motion, and so forth can provide a new perspective on objects and actions. A viewer can see patterns that would not be perceived in the everyday viewing of an object or action. Editing can also present multiple stories for a viewer and move the viewer instantly into the past or future. When rendered creatively, these features can communicate or evoke exhilaration, surprise, and fascination.

These characteristics of motion video have been available to designers for a long time through film and videotape. The new opportunity in the emerging broadband environment will be to add user interaction as a design element. That is, a user can choose options about what to see and control the speed of the action. A user could also maneuver through content and edit together a story or gain a unique perspective about the stored content. This is a general characteristic of interactive television, and it offers new tools for teaching and human development. It can turn a passive learner into an active explorer and creator of content.

**Music and Sound Effects.** Music evokes emotion, reinforces and modifies visual information, and helps to pace action. Sound effects help to identify objects or actions, reinforce or break the pacing established by visuals and music, and provide dramatic nonverbal commentary to storylines. Both music and sound effects deal with rhythms and expectations. They establish a beat or pace that builds expectations and then fulfill the expectation or break it for a dramatic or emotional effect.

As in the case of motion video, the opportunity presented by the new broadband environment is to involve the user or viewer and let him or her interact with the content through music and sound effects. At a simple level, a user could choose to hear music or exclude it. A user could also select background music or choose from a menu of desired emotions (happy, sad, nostalgic) and let the designer choose the music to enhance the desired emotion. Music and sound effects can also be used to enhance the quality of a user's interaction with content; an action by the user could trigger a sound effect or music to strengthen the feeling that the user has actually controlled an object on the screen.

**Screen Resolution, Screen Size, and Number of Screens.** In designed multimedia, enhancements to screen size and screen resolution, as well as the possibility of using multiple screens or multiple windows within a single screen, will provide new tools for designers to increase the dramatic impact of visual information in education as well as entertainment. Designers will be able to show details that were difficult to display in earlier media and to let viewers' eyes move across a field of vision where previously the camera had to move as a surrogate for the eye. These features can be used for dramatic effect or to allow viewers to feel that they are exploring and discovering.

In addition, the windows' environment of multiple images on a single screen, which is now used for menus and other informational purposes, may be used for dramatic and emotional effects, for example, by showing contrasting images in different windows. These effects can be controlled by the designer or the user of a multimedia system. Furthermore, it is likely that many new uses for these features will be discovered and created once they are put in the hands of artists, designers, and educational media producers. Multiple windows are also more feasible in the new home and school environments where computer monitors and television screens are much larger than they were a decade ago.

**Humanizing Help.** The help feature is important in most information systems, both networked and stand-alone systems. In most cases, help consists of written text. If a user wishes to get help from a human being, it is sometimes available by making a telephone call, although the telephone help is rarely integrated directly with the information system.

The new broadband environment will provide an opportunity to design help features with voice, animated graphics, and motion video. This can enrich the flow of information and also provide comfort or support that is difficult to communicate in written text. Furthermore, if it is necessary to provide direct contact with a teacher, trainer, or customer service representative, this can be provided directly through a broadband network and could include video as well as audio contact.

**Hybrid Multimedia Systems.** Some services in the new broadband environment will combine elements of person-to-person interaction and person-to-machine interaction. For example, new forms of distance learning might begin by letting students interact with designed elements—graphics and pictures that convey lessons—and then bring a teacher into the program using live video for explanation and discussion. These new forms of distance education might also combine expensive national productions of designed elements and local or regional teachers for live interaction.

## A Research Agenda

While the new broadband environment offers significant opportunities to enhance the use of expressive communications in teaching and human development, there are many questions or uncertainties that need to be addressed. These questions can build on earlier research in computer-mediated communication and virtual reality systems.

**Cross-Cultural Issues.** Cultural differences are the most intriguing and probably the least understood in terms of impact on development within the broadband environment. One reason is that much international research about technology development has focused on economic and policy issues; less has been directed toward social development and behavior (Kerr, 2000). Among the core issues that need to be addressed are how different cultures shape content and use within the broadband environment; what functions broadband serves in the lives of children compared to other media such as television (Yumiko and Yumiko, 2002); what the locations are for broadband access (examples are homes, schools, and mobile settings) and how these influence the services children experience;

and how the characteristics of the new technology interact with language development.

At a practical level, much use of broadband networks by children in many cultures is likely to involve video games. There is a large body of research literature about video games and children (Provenzo, 1991). Much of it has focused on violent video games and their impact on children's behavior. This is an important issue. However, there is a wider set of research questions such as the role of broadband video games in developing problem-solving skills, hand-to-eye coordination, cooperation and competition, and group interaction in different cultural settings. Higher resolutions that are made possible by broadband networks may change the impact of a next generation of video games (Carey, 2002).

Wireless broadband is proliferating in many countries. There may be a tendency to dismiss it as a tool for children's development, much as television was dismissed as a development tool by many educators in the 1950s. Many early uses of the technology by young people seem frivolous, such as sending photos to friends. However, wireless broadband raises questions about children's sense of privacy, identity, interpersonal relations, formation and maintenance of groups, and sense of space. Furthermore, wireless broadband may lead to a generation of young people who perceive mobile access to a broad range of communication, information, and entertainment services as essential to everyday life.

**Substitution and New Grammars.** Early in the development of new multimedia services, there is a tendency to try to duplicate a face-to-face environment, for example, to create an electronic classroom that mimics a regular classroom. In this sense, engineers and designers often apply a substitution model in creating new systems. This is understandable and appropriate—up to a point. Users of new systems typically acquire them because they can accomplish tasks that were accomplished formerly in a face-to-face setting, and they apply old habits to the new situation. However, the new multimedia service becomes a means of communication unto itself over time. New patterns of behavior form, and the new service becomes a complement to the face-to-face mode rather than a substitute. As this happens, a new "grammar" of interaction forms, but this takes a while to work itself out. For example, we do not think of a telephone conversation as a substitute for a face-to-face conversation, although there is some evidence that many early users thought about and used telephones in this way (Marvin, 1988). Today, the telephone is a vital communication mode unto itself, and the rules or patterns of behavior in a telephone conversation are different in many ways from those in a face-to-face conversation.

This pattern also applies to expressive communication in the new broadband environment. There is a need to understand what habits and expectations users will bring to new systems and to provide an environment where existing face-to-face patterns can be communicated. At the same time, there is a need to conduct research and monitor the new patterns or grammar that form over time and to provide an environment where they can flourish.

There are many additional components to the language structure of new multimedia services. One of these components is metaphor. Metaphors are very useful in dealing with expressive communications because they are analogues for styles and other affective meanings. Furthermore, when the metaphor is captured in a name for the system or service, it can help set expectations about the style of interaction that will take place. For example, when Citibank designed one of its early automated teller (ATM) systems, the designers created and tested a "metaphor" for the ATM—Tilly the Teller. Tilly, or the ATM, was a middle-aged woman who knew the customer and was always courteous but never intrusive. The language used by the ATM in interacting with customers was always conversational: "Hello, how can I help you today?" (Connell, 1990). This metaphor not only helped inform the design of Citibank's ATMs but also built a relationship between the machines and customers. Over the years, many bank customers became so comfortable with the machines that they chose them over human tellers for most of their transactions.

Research can play an important role in identifying a metaphor or persona for a system and testing to ensure that the values represented by the metaphor are designed appropriately into the system.

**Alternate and Multiple Channels.** An important issue in services for the new broadband environment is where to place expressive communications. In face-to-face interaction, expressive communications are conveyed in distinct channels that are integrated with other channels in the gestalt of human communication. For example, a gesture is located in a separate channel (body movement) from words (speech), but both are integrated in the human experience of interacting with another person. Furthermore, there is an important temporal element that affects expressive communication. People may be very expressive at socially appropriate times and less so at other times when intense expressive communications are not sanctioned. For example, in the moments before a class starts, rich expressive communications are often sanctioned as part of "greetings" behavior. Once the class begins, the intensity of expressive behavior is often reduced as a teacher moves into a more digital explanatory mode.

In new multimedia services for broadband environments, it may be possible to locate expressive communication in a separate window, a separate screen, or other channels within the system. Also, expressive communications may be encouraged at certain times and restricted at other times; for example, in an education application, a session might open and close with a social period in which users are encouraged to exchange (and the system helps to convey) casual chitchat, while at other points, the education agenda as well as the system's mode of operation may restrict expressive communications.

There is a strong body of literature on ways to manage these elements in earlier media such as video teleconferences (Johansen, 1984). However, the range of options is now much greater, and therefore the need arises to reexamine how best to manage system elements and human factors in new multimedia services for education and human development.

**Narrowband Versus Broadband.** There has been a good deal of research on the relative effectiveness of narrowband versus broadband channels for tasks such as distance education, for example, whether audio is sufficient or video is necessary to teach social studies. These are important questions, but viewed over a longer time frame, the research questions may change. If we assume that new broadband networks will continue to be adopted in homes and schools, then it is important to begin to ask what the most effective way is to convey expressive and nonexpressive communications in a broadband multimedia environment. From a research perspective, we may shift from an inquiry about alternative sensory channels (audio versus video) to an inquiry about the most effective mix of sensory channels and system designs that foster desired outcomes.

There is also an intermediate set of questions and the need for an intermediate strategy. That is, in the near term, system designers may have available to them greater bandwidth than was available in the past but still well short of the broadband environment that will be available in five to ten years, for example, when the Web may be capable of transmitting HDTV signals. How can this increased bandwidth available today be used most effectively, and what strategy can help prepare users for a generation of services that may follow? Might different sections of a screen (say, a window within a larger screen) be displayed with different resolutions? Should the increased bandwidth be used to increase audio fidelity and therefore enhance the expressive features communicated through tone of voice?

**Creating Content.** There is a large set of questions associated with the creation of content and control over broadband systems. In person-to-person communication, how much control should each user have in manipulating system features, for example, panning and zooming a camera? Can software assist users in creating animated graphics for education and human development applications much as software packages now assist users in creating slides and charts? What are the limits to such assistance? Could a teacher with limited production experience create a thirty-minute video with the help of software? Could a user be given too much control of the technology, and could technological gimmicks become a barrier to learning?

In person-to-machine interactions, who will create education applications, and what value will they place on expressive communications? It is not difficult to imagine that a computer company, a software company, a publisher, and a state education agency might bring very different perspectives to the same application. Similarly, it is not difficult to imagine that applications created largely by computer programmers, educators, or artists might be presented quite differently.

## Obstacles and Opportunities

There is a significant obstacle to the development of expressive communications in the new broadband environment: expressive communication is not likely to surface in surveys of user needs and wants. People do not think about expressive communications. Even if pressed, they find it hard to talk about expressive communications. Those who develop new systems may understand the value and functions of expressive communications. However, this is likely to vary by the type of application and the cultural settings where they are used.

When budget issues arise, strong values are placed on productivity and cost savings. Expressive communications do not serve either value directly. Expressive communications support the exchange of affective and relational meaning. In this sense, they can support the formation and maintenance of teams and creativity that are crucial to human development. In addition, expressive communications can help to create a social network among people who are geographically separated. These values are recognized as important, but they are not often the driving forces behind system development.

In education settings, cost savings and achievement are important values. Expressive communications can contribute to the latter, but the relationship is indirect. The qualities of a teacher that inspire and motivate students are in part affective and relational. Furthermore, expressive communications can help students relate to other students who are spatially separated—in another building nearby or even another state.

The educational potential of the new broadband environment is not just to recreate face-to-face environments but also to give students control over content in the new environment and teach them about visual literacy generally (Messaris, 1997). They can provide new tools to educate and inform learners about how perception of visual reality functions in the everyday world.

The value of expressive communications has long been recognized by the entertainment industry, even though those in that industry use different terms to describe this type of communication. The entertainment industry may also be the first to bring these qualities to the new broadband environment. In the past, qualitative enhancements to consumer electronics, such as color television and high-fidelity sound, have been well received by consumers and enhanced the creative environment for artists. Higher-resolution screens, video windows, and other advances in the new broadband environment will expand the expressive capabilities of artists and designers. The question is whether this will provide a base for educational applications by bringing down costs and spreading the technology widely in homes and schools.

The opportunities for education and human development to ride on the coattails of entertainment applications must be tempered by past experiences with other technologies. In the case of radio, television, and video games, the rich potential to use these new media for education was stymied, at least initially, by commercial forces at work in the marketplace, weak interest by the education establishment, and a lack of resources to develop new educational applications (Carey, 1991). It remains unclear whether the past will be a prologue for education and human development in the new broadband environment. Perhaps what we need is a significant international effort to research the developmental needs of a new generation across many cultures, assess how these can be met in the emerging broadband environment, and produce those tools and services. There is a precedent. In the 1960s, the Ford and Markle Foundations supported a major research and development effort that led to the television series *Sesame Street* and had a significant impact on children's television. A similar vision is needed now for the emerging broadband environment, with a more international focus.

## References

Arnheim, R. *Art and Visual Perception*. Berkeley: University of California Press, 1971.

Bateson, G. "Communication." In N. McQuown (ed.), *The Natural History of an Interview*. Chicago: University of Chicago Press, 1968.

Biocca, F. "Communications Within Virtual Reality: Creating a Space for Research." *Journal of Communication*, 1992, 42(4), 5–22.

Birdwhistell, R. *Kinesics and Context*. Philadelphia: University of Pennsylvania Press, 1969.

Cairncross, F. *The Death of Distance: How the Communications Revolution Will Change Our Lives*. London: Orion, 1997.

Carey, J. "Plato at the Keyboard: Telecommunications Technology and Education Policy." *Annals of the American Academy of Political and Social Science*, 1991, 14, 11–21.

Carey, J. *Content and Services for Next Generation Wireless Networks*. New York: Columbia Institute For Tele-Information, 2002.

Connell, E. "Research and Design for New Banking Terminals." In P. Holmlov (ed.), *Telecommunications Use and Users*. Stockholm: Stockholm School of Economics, 1990.

Forlano, L. *Wireless Time, Space, Freedom: Japanese Youth and Mobile Mania*. Philadelphia: University of Pennsylvania Digital Media Conference, 2003.

Hopkins, J. "Other Nations Zip by USA in High-Speed Net Race." *USA Today*, Jan. 19, 2004, p. B-1.

Johansen, R. *Teleconferencing and Beyond: Communication in the Office of the Future*. New York: McGraw-Hill, 1984.

Johnson, J. *Interface Culture: How Technology Transforms the Way We Create and Communicate*. New York: Basic Books, 1997.

Kendon, A. "Kinesics." In E. Barnouw (ed.), *International Encyclopedia of Communications*. New York: Oxford University Press, 1989.

Kerr, A. "Media Diversity and Cultural Identities." *New Media and Society*, 2000, 2, 286–312.

Marvin, C. *When Old Technologies Were New*. New York: Oxford University Press, 1988.

Messaris, P. "Visual Intelligence and Analogical Thinking." In J. Flood, S. Heath, and D. Lapp (eds.), *Handbook of Research on Teaching Literacy Through the Communicative Arts*. Old Tappan, N.J.: Macmillan, 1997.

Noam, E., Groebel, J., and Gerbarg, D. *Television over the Internet*. Mahwah, N.J.: Erlbaum, 2002.

Provenzo, E. *Video Kids: Making Sense of Nintendo.* Cambridge, Mass.: Harvard University Press, 1991.

Reeves, B., and Nass, C. *The Media Equation: How People Treat Computers, Television and New Media Like Real People and Places.* Cambridge: Cambridge University Press, 1996.

Rheingold, H. *Virtual Reality.* New York: Summit Books, 1991.

Soukup, C. "Building a Theory of Multi-media CMC." *New Media and Society,* 2000, 2, 407–425.

Turkle, S. "Computer Culture." In M. Greenberger (ed.), *MultiMedia in Review.* Santa Monica, Calif.: Voyager Company, 1992.

Yumiko, T., and Yumiko, H. "Television as a Diversion Device." *NHK Broadcasting Studies,* 2002, no. 1, 21–50.

*JOHN CAREY is professor of communications and media management at Fordham University's Business Schools.*

3

*How do children and adults learn to use computers? What developmental processes are involved in learning to use computers? This chapter reviews current understanding of these issues and presents empirical studies demonstrating how to advance that understanding.*

# How Children and Adults Learn to Use Computers: A Developmental Approach

*Zheng Yan, Kurt W. Fischer*

What is the relation between information technology and human development? This is one of the big questions for contemporary developmental scientists. An enormous research literature has documented how information technologies shape human development cognitively (Papert, 1980, 1993), socially (Turkle, 1984, 1995), and physically (Harwin and Haynes, 1992). However, how human beings, particularly ordinary children and adults, master information technology cognitively (understanding the Internet, for example), socially (such as building social network), and physically (for example, learning to use a mouse) has not yet been studied adequately and systematically. As a result, dynamic reciprocal interactions between information technology and human development have been often oversimplified as a static one-way process in which information technology controls human beings. While computer scientists are designing human-centered computers that adapt to people rather than the other way around (Dertouzos, 2001), developmental research will soon fall far behind the technological advances if the research continues to focus on how technology affects people rather than on how people interact with technology.

We thank Joshua Smith and Heping Hao for their feedback on the early version of this chapter and Gerald Knezek, Mark Warschauer, Patricia Greenfield, Ronald Anderson, and Willem Pelgrum for their advice on cultural pathways in using computers. This research was supported by grants from Frederick P. Rose and Sandra P. Rose and the Harvard Graduate School of Education.

### Figure 3.1. The Reciprocal Relations Between Information Technology and Human Development

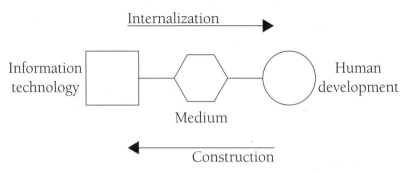

Vygotsky's (1978) social-cultural approach emphasizes that social contexts influence human thinking by an internalization process through cultural media. Piaget's constructivist approach (1983) stresses that human beings actively interact with surrounding environments through a constructive process. These two classic developmental approaches could be adapted to describe specific relations between information technology and human development, as illustrated in Figure 3.1.

Figure 3.1 shows two key features of the relations between information technology and human development (Huston and Wright, 1998; Salomon, Globerson, and Guterman, 1989; Scaife, 1987; Spence, 1999). First, the interaction between information technology and human development is a reciprocal process. The impact of information technology on human development goes through internalization, a process that starts with social contexts, passing through the medium, and eventually being internalized into individual thinking and behaviors. Human beings interact with information technology through construction, a process that starts with individuals' knowledge systems, moves through active accommodation and assimilation, and finally leads to mastering the technology. Second, modern information technology plays a dual role as both part of the social environment (a virtual environment) and part of cultural media. For the internalization process, social contexts have an impact on human development with technology directly (as part of social contexts) and through technology indirectly (as part of the medium). For the construction process, people first need to learn the technology as a cultural tool, and then they will be able to use the tool to interact with social contexts. The processes of both internalization and construction interact with each other simultaneously and constantly, consisting of a dynamic bidirectional system. Thus, these two processes should not be confused or confounded; more important, neither of them should be neglected or downplayed.

With this theoretical framework of information technology and human development interacting with each other reciprocally, this chapter takes a developmental approach to studying the process of construction, particularly the microdevelopmental pathways and cultural pathways of how people learn to use computers, one of the most widely used information technologies. We argue that learning to use computers should be considered an important developmental phenomenon. Studying developmental differences and developmental processes in learning to use computers microdevelopmentally and cross-culturally will generate new empirical data and important research programs. In analyzing how people learn to use computers from the developmental perspective, we hope to move one step further in better understanding the big question: What is the relation between information technology and human development?

## Human Development and Learning to Use Computers

Compared with the substantial literature on how computers change human life, the developmental research literature on how people learn to use the computer is relatively limited. The existing developmental literature has primarily focused on developmental differences across age groups (Calvert, 1994; Scaife and Bond, 1991), but only a little on developmental changes over time (Krendl and Broihier, 1992; Rozell and Gardner, 2000; Subrahmanyam, Greenfield, Kraut, and Gross, 2001). The findings of these studies reflect current understanding of how cognitive development, social development, and physical development play a role in the process of learning to use computers for both children and adults.

**Cognitive Development.** Researchers have studied a variety of topics on how children and adults learn to use computers from the cognitive developmental perspective. Five of the topics are of major importance: (1) developmental appropriateness in children's learning computers (Houston, 1985; Silvern, Williamson, and Countermine, 1988), (2) children's skills of programming or using computer programs such as word processing (Sebrechts, Deck, Wagner, and Black, 1984; Sprigle and Schaefer, 1984), (3) beliefs, conceptions, and representations of computers (Kay and Black, 1990; Krendl and Broihier, 1992; Mioduser, Venezky, and Gong, 1996; Scaife and van Duuren, 1995; van Duuren and Scaife, 1995), (4) perception, memory, and metacognition in learning computers (Calvert, 1994; Clements and Nastasi, 1999), and (5) cyberspace navigation skills (Chiu and Wang, 2000; Head, Archer, and Yuan, 2000; McDonald and Stevenson, 1998; Park and Kim, 2000; Westerman, 1995; Xu, Dainoff, and Mark, 1999; Zizi and Beaudouin-Lafon, 1995).

How adults and children developed their navigation skills in the digital environment is one of the widely studied topics in examining the relation between cognitive development and learning to use computers. Kumpulainen, Salovaara, and Mutanen (2001), for example, investigated a group of elementary students' cognitive strategies in processing multimedia-based information from a science encyclopedia CD-ROM. The results reveal that these students used different cognitive strategies in their navigation processes in the multimedia environment. However, these observed cognitive strategies were rudimentary, with most of them being procedural and product oriented. In another study, Westerink, Majoor, and Rama (2000) investigated seventeen adults' navigational behaviors in multimedia CD-ROM applications as well as their mental models for navigation. Results show that after one hour of a series of exploration and search, only 25 percent of available information items had been explored, and there was little development of their mental models during the study. These two studies suggest that there is no substantial evidence of developmental differences in general navigation skills between children and adults.

Different from the two studies focusing on general navigation skills, Zammit (2000) specifically studied how a group of eleven- and twelve-year-old children understood three types of navigation icons used in CD-ROM programs: pictorial, textual, and a combination of both. The findings of the study indicate that these icons are important tools for children to navigate in a complex cyberspace. Contrary to the common sense of a picture being worth a thousand of words, pictorial icons were no more helpful for navigation than textual ones for these children in the study. The key for effective navigation was generic icons that children were familiar with in their daily life, whether pictorial or textual.

**Social Development.**    Recent studies of how people learn to use computers from the social developmental perspective concern various issues. These issues can be grouped into the following categories: (1) Internet addiction (Davis, Smith, Rodrigue, and Pulvers, 1999; Griffiths, 1997; Young, 1996), (2) social identity and personality (Turkle, 1984, 1995; Ike, 1997), gender difference and stereotype (Rocheleau, 1995; Schott and Selwyn, 2000), (3) computer anxiety and phobia (Weil, Rosen, and Sears, 1987), (4) social interaction and socialization (Crook, 1992; Freeman and Somerindyke, 2001; Lawhorn, Ennis, and Lawhorn, 1996; McKenna, 1999), and (5) life intrusion, privacy, and on-line predators (U.S. Federal Trade Commission, 1998; Bremer and Rauch, 1998).

The Internet loneliness literature (Gross, Juvonen, and Gable, 2002; McKenna, 1999; Kraut et al., 1998) has substantially increased in recent years, suggesting that greater use of the Internet among teenagers is associated with increases in loneliness and depression. However, as an ongoing longitudinal study, the HomeNet project (Subrahmanyam, Greenfield, Kraut, and Gross, 2001) reveals a much more complex pattern.

In this longitudinal study, researchers examined ninety-three families in the Pittsburgh area between 1995 and 1998 to see family use of the Internet. More than one hundred children and adolescents ranging in age from ten to nineteen participated in the study. In the first year of the study, the more hours the children and adolescents used the Internet, the more their psychological well-being declined. The findings of the second year of the study suggest, however, that further use of the Internet was associated with smaller declines or even improvements in psychological well-being. Thus, there existed an interesting shift in social loneliness over two years. Four explanations for this shift in Internet loneliness are given (Subrahmanyam, Greenfield, Kraut, and Gross, 2001). First, this group of children and adolescents may have adjusted themselves and learned to use the Internet more wisely over time rather than excessively, as they did initially. Second, Internet technology has changed dramatically since 1995, especially in terms of easy access and effective use for a wide variety of individuals. Third, the on-line population has grown rapidly over the past few years, and these children can now easily talk to many of their good friends and close relatives through instant messaging or buddy lists. Fourth, early exposure to a novel phenomenon such as the Internet might have a larger impact on behaviors than later exposure. Here, multiple internal factors (for example, children learned to use the Internet wisely over time) and external factors (for example, the Internet technology developed over time) may contribute to the shift in Internet loneliness. While more longitudinal data in this study will be available to show further change in Internet loneliness, one can see how important and revealing it is to study developmental changes over time, even with just two years of investigation.

**Physical Development.** Research literature has reported that learning to use computers involves various aspects of physical development. Active research areas include (1) repetitive strain injury; eye dysfunction and sight deterioration; head, neck, and lower back problems; and other health hazards (Harwin and Haynes, 1992; Lee and Houston, 1986); (2) children's motor skills and their use of mouse, trackball, joystick, helmet-mounted sight, touch screen, eye tracker, keyboard, and other input devices (Lee and Houston, 1986; Scaife and Bond, 1991); (3) the readability of computer screen designs (Dyson and Haselgrove, 2001; Feldmann and Fish, 1988; Grabinger, 1993); and (4) people with special needs, such as visually impaired children and very old computer users (Neuman, 1991; Lawhorn, Ennis, and Lawhorn, 1996; Jacko and others, 2000).

Scaife and Bond's study (1991) on children's developmental differences in using input devices offers an excellent example of studying how to use computers from a physical developmental perspective. They conducted a series of experiments with 228 children ranging from five to ten years old to assess their ability to use four input devices: touch screen, mouse, joystick, and key-push. The findings of the study show that there existed clear developmental differences in using different devices, and younger children had more difficulties using the mouse or joystick than using touch screen and key-push. They found consistent improvement with increasing age, with mastery of all four devices at about eight years of age, consistent with children's bone and muscle development in their fingers, wrists, and arms (Berk, 1996). There were substantial individual variations in using these four devices by children of the same age. Compared with the HomeNet study examining developmental changes over time, this study shows the importance of studying developmental differences across age groups. It helps understanding of how children interact with the computer physically.

**Summary.** To sum up, developmental researchers have studied a variety of topics on both developmental differences and developmental processes in people's learning to use computers. As shown in the existing literature, it is important to study how people learn to use computers from a developmental perspective. This knowledge will help those who develop computer courses as well as computer products that are developmentally appropriate rather than merely user friendly. The literature has also shown that learning to use computers is a complex process encompassing multiple factors and complicated mechanisms. It might be even more challenging for children and adults to learn to use computers skillfully than to learn to read or write well.

Much of the previous developmental research has provided a general developmental picture of how people learn to use computers. It has primarily focused on macrodevelopment (long-term changes) instead of microdevelopment (short-term changes) and on major cultures in North America and Europe instead of diverse cultures across the world. This has limited the potential and promise of the developmental research into people's learning to use computers conceptually and methodologically. In the following two sections, we present a microdevelopmental study of learning to use a computer program and then examine across-cultural studies of learning to use computers to illustrate complex microdevelopmental pathways and diverse cultural pathways.

## Complex Microdevelopmental Pathways of Learning Computers

Microdevelopmental analysis is an established method for examining short-term psychological change through intensive observation and careful analysis of specific activities of individual people (Flavell and Draguns, 1957; Granott and Parziale, 2002; Karmiloff-Smith, 1979; Kuhn, Gracia-Mila, Zohar, and Anderson, 1995; Siegler, 1996; Vygotsky, 1978; Werner, 1956). It is an effective method for describing real-time developmental pathways and uncovering emergent developmental patterns. In the study presented here, we employed the microdevelopmental method to examine a small group of students' individual developmental changes for one hour while they learned to use SAS, a widely used statistical program (Yan, 2000; Yan and Fischer, 2002). The findings of the study reveal complex microdevelopmental pathways and suggest interesting microdevelopmental patterns.

**Microdevelopmental Research.** In the study, six graduate students, averaging thirty years of age, used SAS to complete a simple statistical project after they were taught how to use the program: Susan and Tom were beginning computer users, Cathy and Jack intermediate computer users, and Lily and Mark advanced computer users. Prior to the study, none of them had previous experience using SAS. A teaching assistant was present throughout the study and answered each student's questions in a one-on-one tutorial context.

Each student's performance was then assessed with an eight-level microdevelopmental scale:

| Level | Skill Category |
|-------|----------------|
| 1 | Single sensorimotor actions |
| 2 | Sensorimotor mappings |
| 3 | Sensorimotor systems |
| 4 | Single representations |
| 5 | Representational mappings |
| 6 | Representational systems |
| 7 | Single abstractions |
| 8 | Abstract mappings |

This scale was developed based on both dynamic skill theory (Fischer, 1980; Fischer and Bidell, 1998) and a series of empirical studies of micro- and macrodevelopment (Granott, 1993; Knight and Fischer, 1992). It assesses the cognitive complexity of computational performance at eight levels, ranging from very simple to very complex. For instance, if a learner typed "EDIT" and showed that he or she understood EDIT as a command for opening and editing a file, the cognitive complexity of this performance was coded at the level of single representations and assigned a score of 4. Using students' performance scores as the $y$-axis and their steps in completing the statistical project as the $x$-axis, individual microdevelopmental pathways can be plotted to represent each individual's moment-to-moment cognitive footprints while working on the specific cognitive task in a tutorial context.

**Microdevelopmental Pathways.** Figure 3.2 shows individual microdevelopmental pathways for each of the six students. Despite the relatively fixed procedure required by the computational task in the study, each microdevelopmental pathway is very distinctive, manifesting large variations in each student's unique microdevelopmental history. There are at least four major differences among these six microdevelopmental pathways.

First, these pathways vary in level of complexity. On the upper end, some performances approached level 8 (for example, step 23 for Jack), whereas on the lower end, others approached level 3 (step 3 for Susan). Second, these pathways differ in amount of help received during the study. For instance, Cathy received about thirty helps from the teaching assistant, whereas Mark received only four. Third, these pathways are different from each other in number of steps to complete the project. For example, it took Susan about fifty steps to complete the project, whereas it took Tom only twenty-five steps. Fourth, there are large differences in the overall shape of each pathway. Susan's pathway, for instance, was dominated by many quick

**Figure 3.2.  Microdevelopmental Pathways of Six Computer Learners**

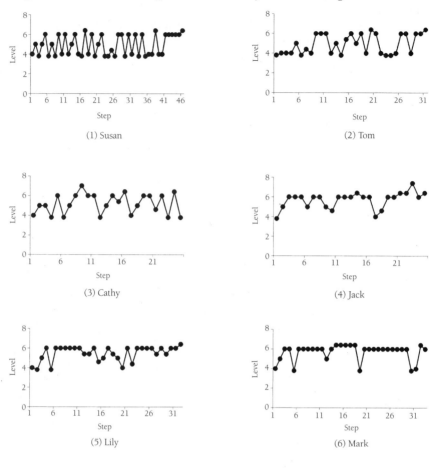

(1) Susan

(2) Tom

(3) Cathy

(4) Jack

(5) Lily

(6) Mark

ups and downs, Cathy's pathway showed longer intervals between ups and downs than Susan's, whereas Lily's pathway showed large fluctuations only in the beginning and the middle.

These pervasive and complicated variations revealed two important patterns underlying the microdevelopmental pathways: (1) the novice-expert pattern, which shows differences related to acquired computer knowledge among the six students, and (2) the transitional pattern, which shows intraindividual changes in ongoing skill acquisition for each student.

*The Novice-Expert Pattern.*  The six students participating in the study represented three types of computer users: Susan and Tom, the two novice users, had started to use computers only a few years ago; Cathy and Jack, the two intermediate users, had a fair amount of knowledge and experience in using computers; Lily and Mark were the expert users, being a Web site designer and an experienced software engineer, respectively. With different computational experience and knowledge, these three types of computer users, ranging from novices to experts, demonstrated distinctive microdevelopmental pathways in learning a new computer program.

As shown in Figure 3.2, microdevelopmental pathways of the least experienced students, Susan and Tom, oscillated with the highest frequency. As a beginning computer user, Susan had more than fifteen wavelike fluctuations, the highest number among the six students. The students with intermediate experience, Cathy and Jack, evidenced oscillations with more relaxed waves and less frequent drops. For the most expert students, Lily and Mark, the pathways started with a few fluctuations and then showed long series stabilized at a high level. As the most experienced student, Mark had only five fluctuations, the lowest among the students. Corresponding closely to their computer knowledge levels, the number of fluctuations in the pathways decreased gradually from Susan to Tom, Cathy, Jack, Lily, and Mark, with Susan's and Mark's pathways as the two extremes of the continuum from novice to expert.

Learning and development is a dynamic construction process in context. When novices begin to learn a new computer program, they need large-scale repeated constructions of their existing knowledge and skills. Thus, novices' microdevelopmental pathways show numerous rapid fluctuations, trying to build an appropriate skill but having difficulty sustaining it. They often need scaffolding from others to construct the skill. As they gradually build new skills, their activities begin to show transient stability, with less extreme and slower fluctuations. After the gradual construction of new skills, people can move more quickly to high-level performance and sustain that performance for longer periods, often without scaffolding from others. Thus, the novice-expert pattern essentially shows how new knowledge and skills are constructed differently by novices, people with intermediate knowledge, and experts.

*The Transitional Pattern.* While interindividual differences among the six students reveal the novice-expert pattern, intraindividual changes within each student show the transitional pattern, indicating emergent construction of new skills. This transitional pattern can be best demonstrated by visually comparing the two microdevelopmental pathways of each pair of students with similar computer experience.

For the two beginning computer users, Susan and Tom, their microdevelopmental pathways show some subtle but visible differences while sharing the same pattern of fluctuations. Tom's pathway appears to have much less fluctuation than Susan's, showing a few high-level performances here and there. This probably means that Tom was slightly ahead of Susan in the process of learning the computational skill, with both illustrating an emerging transition from the most struggling process of learning to a less struggling one.

For the two intermediate-level learners, Cathy and Jack, their microdevelopmental pathways consisted of several scallops, a performance sequence from consecutive progression to consecutive regression (see Fischer and Bidell, 1998; Yan and Fischer, 2002). For example, starting from step 6, Cathy's pathway had three steps of upward progression and then three steps of downward regression, ending this seven-step scallop at step 12. Jack's pathway had a nine-step scallop from steps 17 through 26, including seven consecutive steps of upward progression and three steps of downward regression.

It is not by coincidence that this type of scalloping pattern was observed with the two intermediate-level learners, Cathy and Jack. Similar recurring progression-regression sequences have been found in other microdevelopmental studies (Granott, 1993). As people gradually construct new skills, their activities begin to show temporary stability, with gradual short-term construction and then regression toward a lower level. It is an important indication of an ongoing but not completed development process (Fischer and Bidell, 1998; Fischer and Granott, 1995; Yan, 2000).

As for the advanced users, Lily and Mark, their microdevelopmental pathways show another transitional pattern, having several long sequences of consecutive high-level performances. This pattern did not occur in either the beginning or the intermediate learners. Furthermore, comparing the two pathways, Mark had more and longer clusters of high performance. For instance, from step 7 through step 13, Lily had six steps of consecutive high performance. Mark was the most experienced learner and had two clusters of high performance, one being six consecutive level 6 activities between steps 6 and 13 and another ten consecutive level 6 activities between steps 19 and 29. Thus, the pathways of the two expert students clearly showed a trend toward skill consolidation, while Mark was ahead of Lily in the process of mastering the SAS skill.

**Summary.** This empirical study mainly studied the cognitive process in learning to use a computer program and examined a group of adult computer users rather than children. Even with these constraints, the study provides a complex and informative picture of a real-life learning process where individual computer users interact with computer programs. This demonstrates once again the importance and promise of using new methods and approaches for understanding developmental differences and developmental changes in learning to use computers for both children and adults.

## Diverse Cultural Pathways of Interacting with Computers

Given the complex pathways of learning computers at the microcognitive-individual level as presented in the previous section, are there any differences in people's interactions with computers at the macro-social-cultural level? In other words, do children and adults with different cultural backgrounds use word processing programs or browse Web sites differently? The existing literature on both computer education (Collis and others, 1996; Kozma, 2003;

Pelgrum and Plomp, 1993) and computer design (DelGaldo and Nielsen, 1996; Jacko and Sears, 2003; Nelson, 1990) indicates that not only are there cross-cultural variations in using computers, but also specific pathways of creating these variations are often diverse. This is primarily because both computer users and computer developers inevitably bring different cultures and various psychological characters (for example, age, gender, race, and social class) with them when interacting with computers. Thus, interacting with computers is not culture free but rather a complex process of socialization and enculturation (Greenfield, Keller, Fuligni, and Maynard, 2003; Keller and Greenfield, 2000; Vygotsky, 1978). Although the cross-cultural empirical studies from the developmental perspective are limited, the following analysis focuses on two topics that have been frequently studied: attitudes toward computers and interactions with computers.

**Attitudes Toward Computers.** The empirical literature indicates that cultures affect people's attitudes toward computers, including their perceptions, preferences, expectations, beliefs, dispositions, and anxiety (Rosen and Maguire, 1990; Rosen, Sears, and Weil, 1987; Rosen and Weil, 1995; Weil and Rosen, 1995). There is much evidence of cultural variations in attitudes toward computers, but relatively little is known about pathways of constructing these cultural variations.

Researchers have reported substantial cross-cultural differences in general attitudes toward computers among computer users from different cultures. The populations that have been studied are diverse, including Italian and American university students (Sensales and Greenfield, 1995), Middle Eastern and American college students (Omar, 1992), Chinese and English female undergraduates (Li, Kirkup, and Hodgson, 2001), Japanese, Mexican, and American young children (Knezek, Miyashita, and Sakamoto, 1996), Russian and American school children (Martin, Heller, and Mahmoud, 1992), Romanians and Scottish college students (Durndell and others, 1997), and Chinese and Canadian teenagers (Collis and Williams, 1987).

Given the substantial differences in attitudes toward computers, however, there exists an interesting pattern: computer learners from less technologically advanced cultures tended to have more positive attitudes toward computers than their counterparts in more technologically advanced cultures (Collis and Williams, 1987; Durndell and others, 1997; Martin, Heller, and Mahmoud, 1992; Li, Kirkup, and Hodgson, 2001). This pattern observed across cultures could be associated with the novelty effect, a psychological phenomenon observed within the same culture when individuals who initially have positive emotional responses to the new technology but gradually lose the initial excitement (Knezek, Miyashita, and Sakamoto, 1996; Krendl and Broihier, 1992; Salomon, 1984). In other words, computer learners from less technologically advanced cultures generally have less computer experience and consequently construct a naive but positive attitude to a new technology. Knezek and his associates (Knezek, Miyashita, and Sakamoto, 1996) conducted multiple-country longitudinal studies and confirmed that the novelty effect existed among school students from different cultures. However, they suggested that many other factors, such as changes in students' general attitudes toward schooling, also contributed to the novelty effect.

Besides the cross-cultural differences in attitudes toward computers, the existing literature has documented how these differences were created through specific cultural pathways (Brosnan and Lee, 1998; Knezek, Miyashita, and Sakamoto, 1996; Sensales and Greenfield, 1995). Researchers on computer attitude and computer anxiety, for example, have consistently reported that females generally had higher levels of computer anxiety than males due to the factor that females had less computer experience (Brosnan and Davidson, 1994; Maurer, 1994; Whitely, 1997). However, Brosnan and Lee (1998) found an unusual gender difference that was generated through a different pathway.

Brosnan and Lee (1998) compared the computer attitudes and anxieties of about five hundred undergraduates from the United Kingdom and Hong Kong in 1996. Contrary to the previous literature, the male students from Hong Kong but not from the United Kingdom reported much greater computer anxiety than female students, particularly when anticipating using computers rather than actually using computers. Why did these male students from Hong Kong but not from the United Kingdom have higher levels of anxiety? Why did they report higher levels of anxiety only when they were asked to anticipate using computers but not when they directly interacted with computers?

It seems that the conventional pathway of less computer experience creating higher computer anxiety cannot explain this unique gender difference. There are no differences in using the language, since English is the instructional language at universities in both the United Kingdom and Hong Kong, or in using technologies, since all college students have extensively used computers. Furthermore, the male students from both Hong Kong and the United Kingdom were found to have significantly greater experience than females, but greater computer experience was related to decreased computer anxiety in U.K. males but increased computer anxiety in Hong Kong males.

Brosnan and Lee pointed out a particular pathway, the masculinization of technology, to explain this unique and intriguing phenomenon. The literature indicates that the masculinization of technology has widely taken place within Western cultures (Bem, 1993; Chivers, 1987; Hawkins, 1985). It is generally perceived that computers are more appropriate for males than females and males are more proficient in using computers than females (Colley, Gale, and Harris, 1994; Rosen, Sears, and Weil, 1987; Williams, Ogletree, Woodburn, and Raffeld, 1993). Thus, through the pathway of technology masculinization, the male students from the United Kingdom did not perceive higher computer anxiety. Hong Kong male students, however, had not completely assimilated the view of the masculinization of technology since the Confucian culture still had a profound influence in Hong Kong, but they were fully aware of the challenge of the rapidly developing computer technology due to their substantial computer experience. Thus, through the particular socialization of technology in Hong Kong rather than the conventional masculinization of technology in Western cultures, these Hong Kong male students perceived higher computer anxiety, particularly anticipatory anxiety rather than actual anxiety, even though they had substantially more computer experiences than Hong Kong female students did.

**Interactions with Computers.** Besides cross-cultural differences in attitude toward computers, increasing empirical evidence has shown that cross-cultural differences exist not only in interacting with simple computer features such as icons or menus (Choong and Salvendy, 1998, 1999; Dong and Salvendy, 1999) but also in completing complex computing tasks such as searching Web sites and participating in on-line discussions (Faiola, 2002; Fang and Rau, 2003; Freedman and Liu, 1996; Kim and Bonk, 2002). Choong and Salvendy (1998), for instance, investigated the impacts of cultural differences in recognizing three icon displays (alphanumeric icons only, pictorial icons only, and a combination of the two) between American and Chinese students. The experimental results indicate that American students recognized alphanumeric icons faster and more accurately, Chinese students recognized pictorial icons faster and more accurately, and both American and Chinese students performed well with the combined display.

A few studies have examined diverse cultural pathways of searching information on the Internet (Fang and Rau, 2003; Lightner, Bose, and Salvendy, 1996) and undertaking on-line collaborations (Freedman and Liu, 1996; Kim and Bonk, 2002). Fang and Rau (2003) compared how American and Taiwanese college students searched information from Yahoo! While American students used the standard Yahoo! in English, Taiwanese student used the translated Yahoo! in Chinese. Although the two versions of Yahoo! are similar in layout, content, and structure and both groups had similar good experiences in using the Internet, the keystroke data recorded on the computer and students' satisfaction questionnaire data indicate a significant difference in Internet search sequences and perceived experiences between the two groups of students. Since Yahoo! has not categorized its content in the way that Chinese users are used to, the Chinese students used many more steps and more trials to search information than the American participants did, chose the search method of entering keywords much more rather than browsing categories that are peculiar to them, and perceived many more disadvantages in using Yahoo! to find information.

Accumulated evidence indicates that not only cross-cultural pathways differ in browsing Web sites but also in communicating on-line (Bannon, 1995; Daniels, Berglund, and Petre, 1999; Freedman and Liu, 1996; Kim and Bonk, 2002; Liang and McQueen, 1999). Kim and Bonk (2002) studied cross-cultural differences in on-line collaborative behaviors in Web-based conferences involving 152 undergraduate students and instructors from Finland, the United States, and Korea. Based on qualitative content analyses of computer log data and students' e-mail postings, they found substantial cross-cultural differences in on-line collaborative behaviors: Korean students showed more socially driven behaviors, Finnish students more theoretically oriented ones, and U.S. students more action-based ones, focusing more on seeking or giving solutions.

Although there is increasing evidence indicating cross-cultural differences in how people feel about computers and how they interact with computers, cross-cultural research on using computers is still sparse. Researchers should study more diverse populations (such as young children in school or adults in different professions) rather than mainly college students, use new research methods (such as combining microdevelopmental analyses with cross-cultural research) rather than merely surveys, and explore more underlying processes and mechanisms of computing behaviors (such as longitudinal studies of cultural pathways of using computer programs) rather than just cross-cultural differences.

## Conclusion

The psychological process of learning to use computers can be examined from multidisciplinary perspectives, such as those of cognitive psychology, social psychology, developmental psychology, neurological psychology, educational psychology, industrial psychology, and other disciplines of psychological studies. In this chapter, we have shown that it is valuable to take a developmental approach to understanding how children and adults interact with computers cognitively, socially, and physically. Moreover, it is particularly informative to employ new approaches to study developmental pathways over different time periods, such as microdevelopmental analyses, in different social contexts, such as cross-cultural analyses.

Systematic study of learning to use computers from the developmental perspective in a sense has barely begun. There are many important issues that require timely investigation. For example, a myth about learning to use computers has been popular for years: that it is easy for children to learn to use computers but difficult for old people to learn. However, there have been only anecdotes from daily life and not empirical evidence from scientific research to support this myth. Very little is known about developmental differences between children (especially younger ones) and adults (especially older ones) in learning to use computers. As another example, hundreds of new computer programs have been developed for children and adults to use, but no substantial knowledge exists to guide ordinary computer learners. New research programs ought to be established to compare how children learn to use a wide variety of computer programs for word processing, data analysis, drawing, Web site browsing, and on-line searching; to investigate how children's computer skill development is related to the development of reading, writing, and other fundamental cognitive skills;

and to study how children's specific computer skill development is related to their general cognitive and social development.

Besides substantial knowledge, new research methods and techniques are needed to study how people learn to use computers. It is especially promising when computers provide a powerful tool to store a large number of data, such as publicly accessible databanks; to collect qualitative and quantitative data that are often particularly costly, difficult, and time-consuming to collect, such as large-scale on-line surveys or Web-based experiments; and to process numerical, textual, and graphic data with comprehensive computerized research systems, such as some medical science or neuroscience research systems. In this sense, using the remarkable human-made intellectual tool, the computer, to help understand how human beings master computers will be particularly important for informing practices in education, industry, business, public health, policymaking, and other social domains.

The relation between human development and information technology is reciprocal. Modern information technology has influenced almost every aspect of human life. Both the classic literature and the latest research (Calvert, 1999; Huston and Wright, 1998; Singer and Singer, 2001) have extensively documented and examined this internalization process. Human beings, whether scientific professionals or ordinary laypersons, school children or working adults, individuals with no special needs or people with special needs, actively interact with various information technologies and strive to master them better and sooner. For understanding this construction process, developmental researchers have made initial steps. Developmental scientists, working together with researchers in other psychological fields, will continue to improve our understanding of the bidirectional relationship of information technology and human development.

## References

Bannon, L. J. (1995). "Issues in Computer-Supported Collaborative Learning." In C. O'Malley (ed.), *Computer Supported Collaborative Learning*. Berlin: Springer-Verlag, 1995.

Bem, S. L. *The Lenses of Gender*. New Haven, Conn.: Yale University Press, 1993.

Berk, L. E. *Infants, Children, and Adolescents*. (2nd ed.) Needham Heights, Mass.: Allyn & Bacon, 1996.

Bremer, J., and Rauch, P. K. "Children and Computers: Risks and Benefits." *Journal of the American Academy of Child and Adolescent Psychiatry*, 1998, 37(5), 559–560.

Brosnan, M., and Davidson, M. "Computerphobia: Is It a Particularly Female Phenomenon?" *Psychologist*, 1994, 7(2), 73–78.

Brosnan, M., and Lee, W. "A Cross-Cultural Comparison of Gender Differences in Computer Attitudes and Anxieties: The United Kingdom and Hong Kong." *Computers-in-Human-Behavior*, 1998, 14(4), 559–577.

Calvert, S. L. "Developmental Differences in Children's Production and Recall of Information as a Function of Computer Presentational Features." *Journal of Educational Computing Research*, 1994, 10(2), 139–151.

Calvert, S. L. *Children's Journeys Through the Information Age*. New York: McGraw-Hill, 1999.

Carpineto, C., and Romano, G. "Information Retrieval Through Hybrid Navigation of Lattice Representations." *International Journal of Human-Computer Studies,* 1996, *45*(5), 553–578.

Chiu, C. H., and Wang, F. M. "The Influence of Navigation Map Scope on Disorientation of Elementary Students in Learning a Web-Based Hypermedia Course." *Journal of Educational Computing Research,* 2000, *22*(2), 135–144.

Chivers, G. "Information Technology—Girls and Education: A Cross-Cultural Review." In M. J. Davidson and C. L. Cooper (eds.), *Women and Information Technology.* New York: Wiley, 1987.

Choong, Y. Y., and Salvendy, G. "Designing of Icons for Use by Chinese in Mainland China." *Interacting with Computers,* 1998, *9,* 417–430.

Choong, Y. Y., and Salvendy, G. "Implications for Design of Computer Interfaces for Chinese Users in Mainland China." *International Journal of Human Computer Interaction,* 1999, *11,* 29–46.

Clements, D. H., and Nastasi, B. K. "Metacognition, Learning and Educational Computer Environments." *Information Technology in Childhood Education Annual,* 1999, *10,* 5–38.

Colley, A., Gale, M., and Harris, T. "Effects of Gender Role Identity and Experience on Computer Attitude Components." *Journal of Educational Computing Research,* 1994, *10*(2), 129–137.

Collis, B. A., and others. *Children and Computers in School.* Mahwah, N.J.: Erlbaum, 1996.

Collis, B. A., and Williams, R. L. "Cross-Cultural Comparison of Gender Differences in Adolescents' Attitudes Toward Computers and Selected School Subjects." *Journal of Educational Research,* 1987, *81*(1), 17–27.

Crook, C. "Cultural Artifacts in Social Development: The Case of Computers." In H. McGurk (ed.), *Childhood Social Development: Contemporary Perspectives.* Mahwah, N.J.: Erlbaum, 1992.

Daniels, M., Berglund, A., and Petre, M. "Reflections on International Projects in Undergraduate CS Education." *Computer Science Education,* 1999, *9*(3), 256–267.

Davis, S. F., Smith, B. G., Rodrigue, K., and Pulvers, K. "An Examination of Internet Usage on Two College Campuses." *College Student Journal,* 1999, *33*(2), 257–260.

DelGaldo, E., and Nielsen, J. *International User Interfaces.* New York: Wiley, 1996.

Dertouzos, M. L. *The Unfinished Revolution: Human-Centered Computers and What They Can Do for Us.* New York: HarperCollins, 2001.

Dong, J., and Salvendy, G. "Designing Menus for the Chinese Population: Horizontal or Vertical?" *Behaviour and Information Technology,* 1999, *6,* 467–471.

Durndell, A., and others. "Gender and Computing: West and East Europe." *Computers in Human Behavior,* 1997, *13*(2), 269–280.

Dyson, M. C., and Haselgrove, M. "The Influence of Reading Speed and Line Length on the Effectiveness of Reading from Screen." *International Journal of Human Computer Studies,* 2001, *54*(4), 585–612.

Faiola, A. "A Visualization Pilot Study for Hypermedia: Developing Cross-Cultural User Profiles for New Media Interfaces." *Journal of Educational Multimedia and Hypermedia,* 2002, *11*(1), 51–70.

Fang, X., and Rau, P.L.P. "Culture Differences in Design of Portal Sites." *Ergonomics,* 2003, *46*(1–3), 242–254.

Feldmann, S. C., and Fish, M. C. "Reading Comprehension of Elementary, Junior High and High School Students on Print vs. Microcomputer-Generated Text." *Journal of Educational Computing Research,* 1988, *4*(2), 159–166.

Fischer, K. W. "A Theory of Cognitive Development: The Control and Construction of Hierarchies of Skills." *Psychological Review,* 1980, *6,* 477–531.

Fischer, K. W., and Bidell, T. R. "Dynamic Development of Psychological Structures in Action and Thought." In R. M. Lerner (ed.), *Handbook of Child Psychology,* Vol. 1: *Theoretical Models of Human Development.* (5th ed.) New York: Wiley, 1998.

Fischer, K. W., and Granott, N. "Beyond One-Dimensional Change: Parallel, Concurrent, Socially Distributed Processes in Learning and Development." *Human Development,* 1995, *38,* 302–314.

Flavell, J. H., and Draguns, J. "A Microgenetic Approach to Perception and Thought." *Psychological Bulletin,* 1957, *54,* 197–217.

Freedman, K., and Liu, M. "The Importance of Computer Experience, Learning Processes, and Communication Patterns in Multicultural Networking." *Educational Technology Research and Development,* 1996, *44*(1), 43–59.

Freeman, N. K., and Somerindyke, J. "Social Play at the Computer: Preschoolers Scaffold and Support Peers' Computer Competence." *Information Technology in Childhood Education Annual,* 2001, *13,* 203–213.

Grabinger, R. S. "Computer Screen Designs: Viewer Judgments." *Educational Technology Research and Development,* 1993, *41*(2), 35–73.

Granott, N. "Microdevelopment of Co-Construction of Knowledge During Problem Solving: Puzzled Minds, Weird Creatures and Wuggles." Unpublished doctoral dissertation, MIT, 1993.

Granott, N., and Parziale, J. (eds.). *Microdevelopment: Transition Processes in Development and Learning.* Cambridge: Cambridge University Press, 2002.

Greenfield, P. M., Keller, H., Fuligni, A., and Maynard, A. "Cultural Pathways Through Universal Development." *Annual Review of Psychology,* 2003, *54*(1), 461–491.

Griffiths, M. "Psychology of Computer Use: XLIII. Some Comments on 'Addictive Use of the Internet' by Young." *Psychological Reports,* 1997, *80*(1), 81–82.

Gross, E. F., Juvonen, J., and Gable, S. L. "Internet Use and Well-Being in Adolescence." *Journal of Social Issues,* 2002, *58*(1), 75–90.

Harwin, R., and Haynes, C. *Healthy Computing: Risks and Remedies Every Computer User Needs to Know.* New York: American Management Association, 1992.

Hawkins, J. "Computers and Girls: Rethinking the Issues." *Sex Roles,* 1985, *13,* 193–203.

Head, M., Archer, N., and Yuan, Y. "World Wide Web Navigation Aid." *International Journal of Human-Computer Studies,* 53(2), 2000, 301–330.

Houston, E. S. "Making Child Development Relevant for All Children." Paper presented at the Annual Conference of the National Association for the Education of Young Children, New Orleans, La., Nov. 1985.

Huston, A. C., and Wright, J. C. " Mass Media and Children's Development." In I. E. Sigel and K. A. Renninger (eds.), *Handbook of Child Psychology,* Vol. 4: *Child Psychology in Practice.* (5th ed.) New York: Wiley, 1998.

Ike, C. A. "Development Through Educational Technology: Implications for Teacher Personality and Peer Collaboration." *Journal of Instructional Psychology,* 1997, *24*(1), 42–49.

Jacko, J. A., and Sears, A. (eds.). *The Human-Computer Interaction Handbook: Fundamentals, Evolving Technologies, and Emerging Applications.* Mahwah, N.J.: Erlbaum, 2003.

Jacko, J. A., and others. "Using Electroencephalogram to Investigate Stages of Visual Search in Visually Impaired Computer Users: Preattention and Focal Attention." *International Journal of Human-Computer Interaction,* 2000, *12*(1), 135–150.

Karmiloff-Smith, A. "Micro- and Macro-Developmental Changes in Language Acquisition and Other Representational Systems." *Cognitive Science,* 1979, *3,* 91–118.

Kay, D. S., and Black, J. B. "Knowledge Transformations During the Acquisition of Computer Expertise." In S. P. Robertson and W. W. Zachary (eds.), *Cognition, Computing, and Cooperation.* Norwood, N.J.: Ablex, 1990.

Keller, H., and Greenfield, P. M. "History and Future of Development in Cross-Cultural Psychology." *Journal of Cross-Cultural Psychology,* 2000, *31*(1), 52–62.

Kim, K. J., and Bonk, C. J. "Cross-Cultural Comparisons of Online Collaboration." *Journal of Computer Mediated Communication,* 2002, *8*(1). [http://www.ascusc.org/jcmc/vol8/issue1/kimandbonk.html].

Knezek, G. A., Miyashita, K. T., and Sakamoto, T. "Information Technology from the Child's Perspective." In B. A. Collis and others (eds.), *Children and Computers in School*. Mahwah, N.J.: Erlbaum, 1996.

Knight, C. C., and Fischer, K. W. "Learning to Read Words: Individual Differences in Developmental Sequences." *Journal of Applied Developmental Psychology*, 1992, *13*, 377–404.

Koehler, M. J., and Lehrer, R. "Designing a Hypermedia Tool for Learning About Children's Mathematical Cognition." *Journal of Educational Computing Research*, 1998, *18*(2), 123–145.

Kozma, R. B. (ed.). *Technology, Innovation, and Educational Change: A Global Perspective*. Washington, D.C.: International Society for Technology Education, 2003.

Kraut, R., Kiesler, S., Boneva, B., Cummings, J., Helgeson, V., and Crawford, A. M. "Internet Paradox Revisited." *Journal of Social Issues*, 2002, *58*(1), 49–74.

Kraut, R., Patterson, M., Lundmark, V., Kiesler, S., Mukophadhyay, T., and Scherlis, W. "Internet Paradox: A Social Technology That Reduces Social Involvement and Psychological Well-being?" *American Psychologist*, 1998, *53*(9), 1017–1031.

Krendl, K. A., and Broihier, M. "Student Responses to Computers: A Longitudinal Study." *Journal of Educational Computing Research*, 1992, *8*(2), 215–227.

Kuhn, D., Gracia-Mila, M., Zohar, A., and Anderson, C. *Strategies of Knowledge Acquisition*. Monograph no. 60. Society for Research in Child Development, 1995.

Kumpulainen, K., Salovaara, H., and Mutanen, M. "The Nature of Students' Sociocognitive Activity in Handling and Processing Multimedia-Based Science Material in a Small Group Learning Task." *Instructional Science*, 2001, *29*(6), 481–515.

Lawhorn, T., Ennis, D., and Lawhorn, D. C. "Senior Adults and Computers in the 1990s." *Educational Gerontology*, 1996, *22*(2), 193–201.

Lee, M. W., and Houston, E. S. "The Advantages and Disadvantages of Microcomputers in Early Childhood Education." *Early Child Development and Care*, 1986, *23*(4), 263–281.

Li, N., Kirkup, G., and Hodgson, B. "Cross-Cultural Comparison of Women Students' Attitudes Toward the Internet and Usage: China and the United Kingdom." *Cyber Psychology and Behavior*, 2001, *4*(3), 415–426.

Liang, A., and McQueen, R. J. "Computer Assisted Adult Interactive Learning in a Multi-Cultural Environment." *Adult Learning*, 1999, *11*(1), 26–29.

Lightner, N. J., Bose, I., and Salvendy, G. "What Is Wrong with the World Wide Web? A Diagnosis of Some Problems and Prescription of Some Remedies." *Ergonomics*, 1996, *39*, 995–1004.

MacKenzie, I. S. "Fitts' Law as a Research and Design Tool in Human-Computer Interaction." *Human-Computer Interaction*, 1992, *7*(1), 91–139.

Martin, D., Heller, R., and Mahmoud, E. "American and Soviet Children's Attitudes Towards Computers." *Journal of Educational Computing Research*, 1992, *8*(2), 155–185.

Maurer, M. M. "Computer Anxiety Correlates and What They Tell Us: A Literature Review." *Computers in Human Behaviour*, 1994, *10*(3), 369–376.

McDonald, S., and Stevenson, R. J. "Navigation in Hyperspace: An Evaluation of the Effects of Navigational Tools and Subject Matter Expertise on Browsing and Information Retrieval in Hypertext." *Interacting with Computers*, 1998, *10*(2), 129–142.

McKenna, K.Y.A. "The Computers That Bind: Relationship Formation on the Internet." 1999.

Mioduser, D., Venezky, R. L., and Gong, B. "Students' Perceptions and Designs of Simple Control Systems." *Computers in Human Behavior*, 1996, *12*(3), 363–388.

Nelson, J. *Designing User Interfaces for International Use: Advances in Human Factors/Ergonomics*. Amsterdam: Elsevier Science, 1990.

Neuman, D. "Learning Disabled Students' Interactions with Commercial Courseware: A Naturalistic Study." *Educational Technology Research and Development,* 1991, *39*(1), 31–49.

Omar, M. "Attitudes of College Students Towards Computers: A Comparative Study in the United States and the Middle East." *Computers in Human Behaviour,* 1992, *8*(2–3), 249–257.

Papert, S. *Mindstorms: Children, Computers, and Powerful Ideas.* New York: Basic Books, 1980.

Papert, S. *The Children's Machine: Rethinking School in the Age of the Computer.* New York: Basic Books, 1993.

Park, J., and Kim, J. "Contextual Navigation Aids for Two World Wide Web Systems." *International Journal of Human-Computer Interaction,* 2000, *12*(2), 193–217.

Pelgrum, W., and Plomp, T. (eds.). *The IEA Study of Computers in Education: Implications of an Innovation in Twenty-One Education Systems.* New York: Pergamon, 1993.

Piaget, J. "Piaget's Theory." In P. H. Mussen (ed.), *Handbook of Child Psychology,* Vol. 1: *History, Theory, and Methods.* New York: Wiley, 1983.

Rocheleau, B. "Computer Use by School-Age Children: Trends, Patterns, and Predictors." *Journal of Educational Computing Research,* 1995, *12*(1), 1–17.

Rosen, L., and Maguire, P. "Myths and Realities of Computerphobia: A Meta-Analysis." *Anxiety Research,* 1990, *3,* 175–191.

Rosen, L. D., Sears, D. C., and Weil, M. M. "Computerphobia." *Behaviour Research Methods, Instruments and Computers,* 1987, *19,* 167–179.

Rosen, L., and Weil, M. "Computer Anxiety: A Cross-Cultural Comparison of University Students in Ten Countries." *Computers in Human Behaviour,* 1995, *11*(1), 45–64.

Rozell, E. J., and Gardner, W. L. III. "Cognitive, Motivation, and Affective Processes Associated with Computer-Related Performance: A Path Analysis." *Computers in Human Behavior,* 2000, *16*(2), 199–222.

Salomon, G. "Computers in Education: Setting a Research Agenda." *Educational Technology,* 1984, *24,* 7–11.

Salomon, G., Globerson, T., and Guterman, E. "The Computer as a Zone of Proximal Development: Internalizing Reading: Related Metacognitions from a Reading Partner." *Journal of Educational Psychology,* 1989, *81*(4), 620–627.

Scaife, M. "The Need for Developmental Theories in Cognitive Science: Children and Computing Systems." In C. Julie and C. Crook (eds.), *Computers, Cognition and Development: Issues for Psychology and Education.* Oxford, England: Wiley & Sons (pp. 281–293), 1987.

Scaife, M., and Bond, R. "Developmental Changes in Children's Use of Computer Input Devices." *Early Child Development and Care,* 1991, *69,* 19–38.

Scaife, M., and van Duuren, M. "Do Computers Have Brains? What Children Believe About Intelligent Artifacts." *British Journal of Developmental Psychology,* 1995, *13*(4), 367–377.

Schott, G., and Selwyn, N. "Examining the 'Male, Antisocial' Stereotype of High Computer Users." *Journal of Educational Computing Research,* 2000, *23*(3), 291–303.

Sensales, G., and Greenfield, P. "Attitudes Towards Computers, Science and Technology: Across Cultural Comparison Between Students in Rome and Los Angeles." *Journal of Cross-Cultural Psychology,* 1995, *26*(3), 229–242.

Siegler, R. S. *Emerging Minds: The Process of Change in Children's Thinking.* New York: Oxford University Press, 1996.

Silvern, S. B., Williamson, P. A., and Countermine, T. M. "Young Children's Interaction with a Microcomputer." *Early Child Development and Care,* 1988, *32*(1–4), 23–35.

Singer, D.G.E., and Singer, J.L.E. *Handbook of Children and the Media.* Thousand Oaks, Calif.: Sage, 2001.

Spence, R. "A Framework for Navigation." *International Journal of Human-Computer Studies,* 1999, *51*(5), 919–945.

Sprigle, J. E., and Schaefer, L. "Age, Gender and Spatial Knowledge Influences on Preschoolers' Computer Programming Ability." *Early Child Development and Care,* 1984, *14*(3–4), 243–250.

Subrahmanyam, K., Greenfield, P., Kraut, R., and Gross, E. "The Impact of Computer Use on Children's and Adolescents' Development." *Applied Developmental Psychology,* 2001, *22,* 7–30.

Turkle, S. *The Second Self: Computers and the Human Spirit.* New York: Simon & Schuster, 1984.

Turkle, S. *Life on the Screen: Identity in the Age of the Internet.* New York: Simon & Schuster, 1995.

U.S. Federal Trade Commission. *Privacy Online: A Report to Congress.* Washington, D.C.: Federal Trade Commission, 1998.

van Duuren, M. A., and Scaife, M. "How Do Children Represent Intelligent Technology?" *European Journal of Psychology of Education,* 1995, *10*(3), 289–301.

Vygotsky, L. S. *Mind in Society.* Cambridge, Mass.: Harvard University Press, 1978. (Original work published 1935.)

Weil, M., and Rosen, L. "The Psychological Impact of Technology from a Global Perspective: A Study of Technological Sophistication and Technophobia in University Students from Twenty-Three Countries." *Computers in Human Behaviour,* 1995, *11*(1), 95–133.

Weil, M. M., Rosen, L. D., and Sears, D. C. "The Computerphobia Reduction Program: Year 1. Program Development and Preliminary Results." *Behavior Research Methods, Instruments, and Computers,* 1987, *19*(2), 180–184.

Werner, H. "Microgenesis and Aphasia." *Journal of Abnormal and Social Psychology,* 1956, *52,* 347–353.

Westerink, J.H.D.M., Majoor, B.G.M.M., and Rama, M. D. "Interacting with Infotainment Applications: Navigation Patterns and Mental Models." *Behaviour and Information Technology,* 2000, *19*(2), 97–106.

Westerman, S. J. "Computerized Information Retrieval: Individual Differences in the Use of Spatial vs. Nonspatial Navigational Information." *Perceptual and Motor Skills,* 1995, *81*(3), 771–786.

Whitely, B. "Gender Differences in Computer-Related Attitudes and Behaviour: A Meta-Analysis." *Computers in Human Behaviour,* 1997, *13*(1), 1–22.

Williams, S., Ogletree, S., Woodburn, W., and Raffeld, P. "Gender Roles, Computer Attitudes and Dyadic Computer Interaction Performance in College Students." *Sex Roles,* 1993, *29*(7/8), 515–525.

Xu, W., Dainoff, M. J., and Mark, L. S. "Facilitate Complex Search Tasks in Hypertext by Externalizing Functional Properties of a Work Domain." *International Journal of Human-Computer Studies,* 1999, *11*(3), 201–229.

Yan, Z. "Dynamic Analysis of Microdevelopment in Learning a Computer Program." Unpublished doctoral dissertation, Harvard University, 2000.

Yan, Z., and Fischer, K. W. "Always Under Construction: Dynamic Variations in Adult Cognitive Development." *Human Development,* 2002, *45,* 141–160.

Young, K. S. "Psychology of Computer Use: XL. Addictive Use of the Internet: A Case That Breaks the Stereotype." *Psychological Reports,* 1996, *79*(3), 899–902.

Zammit, K. "Computer Icons: A Picture Says a Thousand Words. Or Does It?" *Journal of Educational Computing Research,* 2000, *23,* 217–231.

Zizi, M., and Beaudouin-Lafon, M. "Hypermedia Exploration with Interactive Dynamic Maps." *International Journal of Human-Computer Studies,* 1995, *43*(3), 441–464.

*Zheng Yan* is an assistant professor of educational psychology at the State University of New York at Albany.

*Kurt W. Fischer* is Charles Bigelow Professor of Education and director of the brain and education concentration at Harvard University Graduate School of Education.

*Connecting the debates in social theory with examples from recent advertising that draw on meanings and images of children, this chapter shows how some recent representations of childhood that engage explicitly with new information technologies are forms of economically invested socialization, precisely through their subscription to changing discourses of emotions.*

# Emotional Capital and Information Technologies in the Changing Rhetorics Around Children and Childhoods

*Ángel J. Gordo López, Erica Burman*

Throughout the history of Western culture, special attention has been devoted to the study and understanding of emotions. Notwithstanding considerable cultural and historical specificities, Western culture since the Enlightenment has treated reason as the foundation of morality and progress. Emotions and their synonyms, such as *passion, instincts,* and *sexuality,* were commonly associated with those who failed to fit the model of Western (culturally masculine) rationality: children and "primitives," women, the working class, and mad people (Birke, 1982; Burman, 1999a, 1999b, 2001). All of these nonnormative populations have been depicted as potentially dangerous and a threat to moral and social order.

A remarkable exception can be found in Aristotle's work (1941), which accorded a vital role to emotions in his account of ethics and politics. He was concerned with the ways in which emotions could be "educated" to become a powerful rhetoric means. Interestingly, Aristotle regarded emotions as embedded within individuals, as well as in social interaction. He also saw close connections between emotions, communication, and the art of politics or rhetoric.

Notwithstanding the fact that Aristotle's studies received sustained attention in medieval universities and empiricist philosophers, the positivist hegemony of the late nineteenth century displaced the study of emotional life as falling outside the remit of legitimate scientific concern. In many instances, emotion, like sexuality, was considered tantamount to disorder

NEW DIRECTIONS FOR CHILD AND ADOLESCENT DEVELOPMENT, no. 105, Fall 2004 © Wiley Periodicals, Inc.

by virtue of its link with nature, for nature stood in contrast with civilization and order. As Lutz (1996, p. 151) puts it, "In the West, emotion, like the female, has typically been viewed as something natural rather than cultural, irrational rather than rational, chaotic rather than ordered, subjective rather than universal, physical rather than mental or intellectual, unintended and uncontrollable, and hence often dangerous."

Since the late 1970s, critical social theory has challenged traditional biological and psychological approaches to emotions (Lutz and White 1986; Parkinson, 1995). Like most anthropologists, a number of innovative psychologists have criticized the dominant psychological tradition of laboratory-based experiments (see Svaöek, 2002). Not surprisingly, the main focus of most social research on emotions has been the social and cultural dynamics of emotional life.

It is now widely accepted that emotions ought to be understood as part of a broader cultural matrix (Averill, 1996; Harré, 1986). From this perspective, emotions are not immune from, and cannot be divorced from, cultural influence. Neither, as we shall argue, are current educational, technological, and ideological debates. In this chapter, we address emotionally invested representations of children currently circulating within mass media and advertising campaigns to discuss how such representations can provide a key resource for the analysis of changing forms of subjectivity emerging within the new information society.

## The Effervescence of Emotions

Although prevailing scientific and expert accounts of the past decades devalued emotions in relation to cognition or rational thought (Walkerdine, 1988), a renewed interest in emotion can be seen within recent sociological, psychological, educational, and, among others, marketing strategies. During the 1970s, at a time of major crisis within the welfare state, structural social and class problems became rendered by political discourse into identity categories such as ethnicity and gender (Álvarez-Uría, 1998). Similarly, we will argue that discontent and achievement have now started to be coded in terms of the management and education of emotions.

In this regard, it is worth recalling the importance that influential sociologists such as the British academic (and close adviser to the British prime minister Tony Blair) Anthony Giddens accords emotional life (Giddens, 2000). If, in his previous studies (Giddens, 1992), he identified resemblances between therapeutic work and intimate relationships, more recently he has drawn parallels between "emotional communication" and democratic systems in Western societies. Giddens understands emotional communication as establishing the common ground for a variety of friendship, familial, sexual, and love relations. But what is especially striking is the way Giddens envisages emotional communication as the key way to deal with the vast range of problems within Western democracies.

There are other fronts where emotions are acquiring a strong presence within a variety of educational and human resource practices. Moreover, this is where links with the discipline of psychology come to the fore. Although the epithet *emotional intelligence* came into the public domain only after the publication of Daniel Goleman's best-selling book of this title (1995), the term has its roots in the concept of social intelligence, which was defined by Thorndike (1920, p. 228) as "the ability to understand and manage men and women, boys and girls—to act wisely in human relations." Indeed, it has come to mean the ability to relate to and understand people. Emotional intelligence, in contrast, "is a type of social intelligence that involves the ability to monitor one's own and others' emotions, to discriminate among them, and to use the information to guide one's thinking and actions" (Mayer and Salovey, 1993, p. 433).

Like Giddens, Goleman sees the education and control of emotional intelligence as a way to prevent and sort out a wide range of personal and social problems. A key theme of the book concerns the importance of dealing with our lack of control over our emotions. If Giddens considers emotional communication to be a way of democratizing democracy, Goleman regards emotional literacy and the management of irrationality as a major means to prevent collective emotional crisis. Moreover, he makes grand claims for its applications as the way to deal with such intractable social problems as street and domestic violence, educational failure, and family crisis.

Contemporary philosophers (Elster, 1999; Marinas, 1996) and social scientists are just beginning to address the relationship between sentiments, and in particular emotional intelligence, to other phenomena, including leadership and management (Ashforth and Humphrey, 1995). An example of the managerial interest in emotional intelligence is well illustrated by the work of Goleman, Boyatzis, and MacKee (2002) and the publicity this work has received in the business and employment sections of European newspapers. Drawing on some of the psychological and educational sources identified above, Boyatzis (2003) defines emotional intelligence as a constellation of four abilities: being aware of one's thought and feelings, being capable of emotional self-control and adaptability, having empathy for other people's feelings, and being able to relate to others. Boyatzis suggests that the styles of leadership that are developed according to emotional intelligence allow the good manager to create an atmosphere in which people want both to make and to offer the best of themselves. He identifies the following emotional intelligence traits of "good" managerial practices:

> In the first place, the big leaders. . . . are those people who know how to get the best out of us. . . . Their emotional intelligence is activated by neural circuits and it is translated clearly in actions allowing them to establish resonance with others. . . . The leaders of all types of organisms can be surrounded by teams and resonant cultures to promote emotional intelligence

and to get the best from each person. And they make it into a developing culture of the organization or the social group (which could be a family or a community) [p. 2, our translation].

Like Giddens and Goleman, but with an emphasis on uncertainty and the economically difficult times, Boyatzis (2003) portrays emotional intelligence as an enormous asset among leaders insofar as "we need their hope with regard to the future and the positive energy that contributes to creativity in big organizations, to sustain us and to make us see the light that there is at the end of the tunnel."

Yet notwithstanding the analogy implied between emotionally intelligent leaders and messianic salvation, such managerial styles informing current constructions of emotional intelligence, including ideas for its "actualization" and educability (see Greenberg, Kusche, Cook, and Quamma, 1995), also recall Aristotle's theses on the ways different types of education correspond with the different political systems.

The question that arises here is this: What sort of political systems and forms of control do issues such as emotional communication and emotional intelligence correspond to and endorse? Is emotional intelligence, with its emphasis on self-control and regulation, an appropriate model for the public domain? Or, on the contrary, does it help to bolster new forms of individualization, including assumptions about its neural nature? Moreover, what discursive connections can be identified between this focus on the educability of emotions and representations of childhood within the current information society? We take each of these questions in turn.

## Upping the Rhetorical Stakes: Children and Emotions

Aristotle placed emotions within an overall conception of the development of personality, or what he called character (Robinson, 1996). But while Aristotle treated the emotions as situated within wider social and political perspectives, this was in contrast with modern individualist narratives of liberal development. As a key hallmark of nineteenth-century European thinking, such narratives treated the child, "the primitive," women, and the mentally ill as incomplete or immature versions of the adult, male, rational mind. All else were mere steps on the way to a particular, culturally defined model of maturity. In particular, the developing child, exemplifying the joint qualities of social Darwinism—adaptability and the realization of inherent potential— was invested with key preoccupations of modernity and its teleological economic model of development. Indeed, the child came to personify and naturalize, through the documentation and regulation of its life course, the modern faith in progress. Like the study of primates (Haraway, 1989), the child study movement functioned to foster the conviction that individuals and societies are developing toward some "better," more adaptive, more beneficial form of organization. Hence, Western liberal individualism has produced a modern industrialized state apparatus that is characterized by a panoply of child-watching technologies (from Sully and Gesell onward) that can monitor children developing at the right pace and check progression through designated developmental milestones (Burman, 1998a, 1998b; Rose, 1996).

But as well as connotations of manipulability, the concept of the developing child has produced its alternative set of metaphorics concerned with precisely those qualities that development leaves behind. As with the history of their emergence, romanticism appears as the counterpoint to functionalism. For if the developing child is invested with the hopes of modern economic development, the state from which children develop remains identified with the costs and losses of such efforts. That is, if alienation has come to characterize the dominant affect of those living under the constraints and exertions of the modern state, then childhood has come to symbolize the retroactively constructed, timeless domain of innocence and naturalness from which the modern adult is severed through her or his adaptation to the structures of industrial life. Indeed, Steedman's historical analyses of Western culture (1995) persuasively indicate that from the mid-eighteenth century onward, and coinciding with the emergence of the child protection movement (which at that time was protecting children from labor rather than, as in the current climate, sexual exploitation), the child emerged as the privileged site to configure the emerging form of Western subjectivity, as a self with interiority and history. A structural ambivalence, then, infuses dominant representations of childhood: of lost innocence (with its associations of spontaneity and unself-conscious embodiment) but also of the—perhaps envious—need to hurry away from such forbidden pleasures and distractions. Nostalgia and sentiment are the dominant emotions generated by association with childhood, with key implications for children who fail to fit such idealized representations (Burman, 1999a, 1999b). Thus, the status of children's work and sexuality recur as key sites of contemporary social anxiety as marking a threshold limiting, but also revealing, the limits of, modern Western democratic participation (Burman, 2002, 2003).

In this context of massive emotional investment, the metaphor of childhood has also been subject to all sorts of rhetorics, including those prompted by both market strategies and the politics of warfare. Distinctions between rational politics and irrational emotions, and between the adult and child—and especially between women and children—are ideological constructs, with specific and cultural rhetorical effects. Hence, the profoundly ideological discourse of childhood innocence (in the sense that it is only partially and strategically deployed or acted on) includes as a key motif the claim to priority that children have in times of political conflict. This can be mobilized not only for emotional but also massively destructive, geopolitical aims, which, as Svaôek (2002) points out, do not always result in political change. Indeed, one small indication of the multiple uses of such ideological motifs is indicated by how a strategic essentialism around the children's "needs" has been used to negotiate temporary cease-fires within intractable political conflicts for the delivery of immunization and food and medical supplies to children explicitly on the basis that children are "peace zones" (Burman, 1999a).

In the prewar mass media coverage of the 1990–1991 Gulf War, the U.S. press drew on various propaganda devices to direct public opinion in favor of the war. One of the media campaigns to justify the attack on Iraq included presenting the public with escalating anti-Iraq coverage. At the peak of constructing the justification for war, prowar U.S. media broadcast the news that Iraqi forces had killed babies in incubators in Kuwait City.[1]

This news, which was distributed by the public relations firm Washington Hill and Knowlton, helped to increase public support for the war against Iraq. This mass media justification of war, as the British journalist Maggie O'Kane has documented, was in fact never substantiated by the nurses of Kuwait City hospital. On the contrary, it was later established that the source of this claim was the fifteen-year-old daughter of the Kuwaiti ambassador in Washington, who appeared in Congress claiming to be a nurse but who had actually spent years away from Kuwait. As O'Kane (1997; cited in Mainstream Media, 2001) puts it: "There is always a 'dead babies history' when war justification is at stake," and, we might add, when the purpose is to demonize the enemy and construct a sense of urgency that dispenses with the time required for diplomatic intervention. Moreover, if the murder of children prompts condemnation in most (or all?) cultures regardless of economic, religious, and cultural differences, such rhetorical issues were also at issue—at least in Western imagination in the denials of the North Atlantic Treaty Organization bombing of an Iraqi children's hospital.

With less dreadful yet no less profound consequences, links made between childhood and emotion now form a widespread resource for marketing strategies too. This relationship is elaborated within a wide range of advertisement campaigns, such as those for cell phones. Among these we briefly discuss is the massive advertising campaigns launched by the Spanish company Airtel during 1996 to promote its new SOS services.

Among the most recent services that Airtel promoted in this campaign were the "button Airtel" services, which were advertised on prime-time television slots and written and graphic press. From anyplace and twenty-four hours a day, the client could access a wide range of services or information. By merely pressing a button on the telephone, Airtel puts at the client's disposal an ambulance, roadside automobile repair services, a plumber, or information and services worldwide.[2] This new service was launched with an advertising campaign with the slogan "Mom!" ¡Mamaaa! in the original Spanish.

The campaign took the form of presenting several situations in which adults and children faced a problem or need. Experiencing the sensation of impotence, they scream: "Mom!!" Examples of the situations depicted included a child asking for help when other children snatched his ball on the basketball court, a father feeding baby triplets, and a young woman whose car has broken down on a deserted road. The voice-over offers the solution of using "button Airtel" with the following message:

> Mom! We present the button Airtel. Whatever you need, ranging from changing a wheel for you to booking accommodation in Singapore, we provide it immediately. Because Airtel mobile is much more than a telephone. We give voice. ¡Mamá! Presentamos el botón Airtel. Necesites lo que necesites te echaremos una mano inmediatamente, desde cambiarte una rueda hasta reservarte hotel en Singapur. Porque un móvil Airtel es mucho más que un teléfono. Llevamos la voz.]

The campaign worked to grip the consumer by evoking an infantile stage of helplessness, regardless of age boundaries, with its humorous style aided by the comic-like-style vignettes displayed visually frame by frame (evoking the genre of the graphic novel).

Current lifestyles involve accepting the occurrence of unexpected events (or risk) as well as the need for sudden, almost impulsive but rational, responses (or security). The Airtel campaign conveys the sense of the widespread and pervasive character of risk and corresponding dependency and need for fast solutions. It highlights the ubiquity, immediacy, interactive, and global dimensions that characterize information networks. It also cuts across geographical, age, and cultural distances to connect people's (social and technological) dependencies and emotions by their need for consuming services.

Airtel also can depict itself as caring and responsive, showing striking concern for its clients. The company is able to present itself as identifying problems and then responding by providing resourceful connections to help manage the material, informational, and emotional aspects of life's eventualities. It also offers a commitment to provide this in an era of damaged social fabric and galloping individualism whereby people are ever more needful of affection and emotion "shots," and when the picking and choosing of identities, including the new communicational supports that enhance them, play a key role.

In this changing context, information technologies exhibit a dual dimension: they contribute to constructing and adjusting the changing socioeconomic landscape and facilitate the connection and ordering of everyday actions to remind us of (while also enhancing) the fragile and dependent states to which we are continuously exposed.

This dual dimension is well illustrated by "e-motion," another recent cell phone advertising campaign mounted by Movistar (the cell phone branch of the Spanish communication company Telefónica). Although we will not offer here a detailed analysis of this advertisement (but see Gordo López, 2003), it is worth mentioning the following message that accompanied this campaign: "Allow yourself to be guided by your e-motion. . . . you don't adapt to e-motion, e-motion adapts to you" (Movistar, 2001).

It is not surprising, then, that information technologies, alongside professional psychological and counseling advice services, play an ever more central part in our lives. From this perspective, the impact of the new technologies, far from conflicting with the much discussed crisis in the sense of community and affiliation, is also fed by it. In such a state of affairs, childhood and emotion import new meanings as key social categories that manage and order contemporary relations. In the Airtel example, adults might feel infantilized, in need of new informationally mobile figures, with their extended possibilities of connection and consumption. In addition, Airtel's comic effects of adults seen crying for help with the expression "Mom!" indicate the type of subjectivity to be forged alongside the developing information society.

In such a context, how ought we to understand the current effervescence of emotion? What new inscriptions and rhetorics now surround forms of subjectivity that have traditionally expressed emotions through representations of children?

## Emotional and Technologically Embodied Childhood: The Teletubbies

Debates about children and the mass media have reverberated across a wide range of domains, including the family and schooling. More recently, they have been concerned with the nature of young people's socialization (through video games, mobile phones, and the Internet) and with their vulnerability to "social deviations" (like those connected with role playing, hacking, and pedophilia, for example).

As Buckingham (2000, pp. 7–8) argues, most of debates are about the way the media are implicated in the contested issue surrounding childhood: "On the one hand, they serve as the primary vehicle for these ongoing debates about the changing nature of childhood—and in the process, they undoubtedly contribute to the growing sense of fear and panic. Yet on the other hand, the media are frequently blamed for *causing* those problems in the first place—for provoking indiscipline and aggressive behaviour, for inflaming precocious sexuality, and for destroying the healthy social bonds, which might prevent them from arising in the first place."

The abstraction of childhood, in its different forms and situated representations, allows for it to function as a repository for all sorts of fantasies and moral panics. From this we may well ask, To what extent is it accurate to claim that the distinction between adults and children is disappearing (the so-called death of childhood)? What types of links can be established between these emerging representations around childhood-emotion-information technologies and new strategies of individual and collective government?

The current technocultural imagery is raising awareness of, and indeed marketing, the relational and technological character of our subjectivity. In addition, this consciousness is being articulated across the terrain of the mental, physical, and emotional. Most forms of human-machine symbiosis developed in the early industrial period established a safe but ambiguous distance between our bodies and machines. However, the symbiosis between mental processes and information processes is more complex and exchangeable. There are now new boundaries between technology and subjectivity in which, as Barglow (1994) notes, the Western autonomous self can no longer be taken for granted, and even less so if we consider the increasing demand for the production, including the social and physical incorporation, of information technologies.

Such incorporations are epitomized in the forms and performances of the young children's television program *Teletubbies,* with the central protagonists (of the program's title) portrayed with TV screens located within their tummies and with antennas on their heads. They also display the joyful, tactile, and highly emotional behaviors and speech attributed to preschool children. *Teletubbies* was first broadcast in the United Kingdom in March 1997. This apparently naive and innocent children's TV program was to generate massive and long-standing national debates, as well as to sell worldwide for television and video markets.

Albert Schafer (1999, p. 5), the head of the ARD/ZDF Children's Channel, claimed that this program format "gets away from adapting children's television from the formats of programmes for adults." He also stated that the program "is quite radically tailored to television beginners: with the repetitions, with the slow pace, with the different language levels. There is not only the blah-blah level; but also the correct language level. That alarms people, and this together with the attention associated with it are part of the success."

As Buckingham (1999) indicates, the program combines two parallel traditions in British preschool programming: the child-centered, educative approach characterized by the emphasis on learning through play and the use of songs and rhymes, and the entertainment approach that speaks "more directly to the imagination: they featured anthropomorphic characters in fantasy worlds, and traded in nonsense, repetition and absurd humour" (p. 11). Indeed (perhaps unsurprisingly) most of the controversy surrounding *Teletubbies* reflected ongoing ideological debates on educational standards in the United Kingdom.

Much of the debate among academic experts and educational psychologists centered around whether the program's use of "baby talk," its repetitions and performance, facilitated children's language development or, on the contrary, undermined it. In this regard, the series was caught in the crossfire of debate that was raging about the supposed "dumbing down" of British culture. As White indicates, the vast majority of the complaints focused on the inarticulacy of the characters, their "dumbness" (White, 1999, p. 17): "They say they are slow, silly, banal and incoherent, and that the programme is aimed at children who are really too young to be watching TV at all" (Maggie

Brown, 1997, cited in White, 1999, p. 17). Here it is relevant to note the massive popularity of the characters and merchandise from the program within youth and student culture—whether as a perverse reflection of this "dumbing down" (indicated by the more general infantilization of popular culture; Daly and Wice, 1995) or as a response to the moral outrage it provoked.

In terms of educational issues, *Teletubbies* posed four key economic, cultural, and political questions. The first issue was whether children, depicted as a captive audience, should be kept innocent of the supposed contamination of commerce (as ushered in by the exposure to television in general and all the product-related articles that accompanied the release and success of the *Teletubbies*). *Teletubbies* sold to more than fifty-nine broadcasters around the globe. By 1998, BBC Worldwide, a wholly owned commercial subsidiary of the BBC, had earned well over 55 million sterling pounds from the merchandising articles alone (Buckingham, 1999; White, 1999).

A second related issue concerned questions of cultural bias and accusations of cultural imperialism. In Buckingham's view, such debates suggest that *Teletubbies* was "symptomatic of the `mixed economy' that increasingly characterizes the media environment. It represents a complex interweaving of commercial and public service imperatives and of national and global considerations of existence of contemporary television" (Buckingham, 1999, p. 10; see also Howard and Roberts, 1999; White, 1999).

Third, the program was accused of promoting homosexuality among children. This controversy revolved mainly about the character Tinky Winky. While conservative sectors expressed disapproval of the supposedly queer manners of this character, Tinky Winky (with "his" purple body color and handbag) was soon to become an icon among nonheterosexual communities. The final claim concerned whether the often mildly anarchic quality of the programs, including its surreal or hyperreal quality, was informed by and promoted designer drug culture, a claim that, if sustainable at all, is probably what prompted the youth culture interest (Buckingham, 1999). As Howard and Roberts (1999, p. 19) indicate in relation to the controversy that accompanied the screening of the program in the Australian context, responses "have linked the *Teletubbies* with homosexuality, drug abuse and suchlike."

But who are the Teletubbies? Why do they elicit such divided responses, portraying them as part lovable and yet pejoratively? In what ways can the massive media attention and critique devoted to the screening of *Teletubbies* be related to deeper anxieties and moral panics (Howard and Roberts, 1999) in Anglo-Saxon countries?

Like David Bowie in the 1970s, the Teletubbies come from another planet. Their forms take on strange but appealing familiar features and gestures. At first sight, we can recognize cuddly big-eyed monkey-human-alien-like features with no apparent secondary sexual markers. These lovable creatures with antennas rising from their heads also each have a flap over their "tummies," which, when pulled away, reveals a television screen. They name themselves Laa Laa, Po, Dipsy, and Tinky Winky and are physically differentiated from one another by color (green, purple, red, and yellow), size (1.2 to 1.6 meters), the shape of their antennas, and ways of interacting and talking.

The heated debates that surround the Teletubbies mode of communication and ambiguously sexed bodies are informative of the competing discourses that regulate definitions of childhood in Western societies. We can identify images of the little (but undeveloped) rational adult, alongside the emotional and undeveloped (alien) child; the seemingly nonsexual child, as well as the apparently contradictory representations of the neutral and gendered infant. Here their very "tubbiness," as with children, signifies both the presence of appetites and desires and (within a culture that pathologizes flesh) immaturity. Moreover, the Teletubbies also enjoy forms of self-projection onto adults' mode of communication, both in the sense of simulation but also literally by the screen in their tummies providing the body origin point of the narrative transposition between the pastoral scenes of their play and the other excerpts they show (and replay). Seemingly domesticating Cronenberg's early sinister representation of the ways technology enhances and expresses the voyeurism and fetishism within sexuality in his 1982 film *Videodrome*, the videos projected from their teletummies provide the Teletubbies with trembling (almost masturbatory?) pleasure in the process of projecting these images from their tummies (also, within the narrative of the program, inducting the learning child into the adult reasoning world, since the "educational" stories of the series emanate from there). Here, we should recall how in Western societies, the stomach, or solar plexus area (or "tummy"), has since the early Greeks signified the privileged site for emotions and irrationality, including the locus of authentic feeling.

At the same time, the mediated aspect of the screen can also be understood as a naturalized animistic environment for children developing in the twenty-first century. This environment and the socializing power of the screen (for example, through video games, computers, computer play stations, and cyberpets) has rendered the boundaries between childhood and adulthood open to continuous transgression. They are not related to chronological age but rather appear to be governed by a timeless unconscious developmental pace once we are exposed to the Teletubbies multimedia and the diverse narratives.

Buckingham (1999) argues that the success of *Teletubbies* with young people and adults could be seen as a "form of regression or infantilisation— or at least, as further evidence of the blurring of boundaries between children and adults. . . . This is to imply that, like childhood, adulthood is also a provisional state, which can be defined and constructed in different ways for different purposes. In this context, 'childishness'—like 'youth' before it—is becoming a kind of symbolic commodity, that is marketable to consumers whose biological status places them well beyond the obvious target audience" (pp. 12–13).

What implicit hierarchies are implied by such polemics? Furthermore, in the context of our argument here, what do such debates about the Teletubbies tell us about the complex relations between the embodiment of emotion, childhood, and technology over time?

## Cyborg Productions Overview

If the integration of human and machine has long been dreamed of by different technocratic and industrial regimes, now access to information technology has promoted new types of inquiry into the relations between flesh and technology and between forms of social agency and computer-mediated facilities. Some of these accounts advocate the improvement, enhancement, or even abandonment of biological limitations with the aid of new technological devices. These positions have given further impetus to the revival of discourses around the abandonment of the body, or even of operating outside its biological realm.

At the historical moment when the Human Genome Project and information and communication technologies are saturating our imaginaries, such reflection on the relations between childhood and information technologies might tell us something about the way disciplinary knowledges are shaping the contours of the social sciences. This is alongside another key development, the emergence of the so-called third culture, by which hard scientists in fields such as artificial intelligence, artificial life, fractals, nanotechnology, cellular automata, virtual reality, and cyberspace "are taking the place of the traditional intellectuals in rendering visible the deeper meanings of our lives, redefining who and what we are" (Brockman, 1995, p. 2). This broader scenario is too broad and too complex for us to provide a precise analysis here. However, it is important to understand these as forming the conditions for the increasing interest in computer-child encounters and relations.

Huhtamo (1999) highlights the way discourse on automation emerged with other discourses related to consumerism and modernity after World War II. The mass media played an important part in this process in both publicizing and providing access to such new technological developments. The first public appearance of computers "took place in television shows, newspaper cartoons and popular science stories" (Huhtamo, 1999, p. 160). It is noteworthy that, for instance, "there were game shows on TV featuring huge room-sized 'giant brains' for whom a human (often a grandmother or a child) was allowed to pose questions." In this sense, the child appeared as a suitable interface to humanize the new technological presence that was until then associated with destruction and fear. The child was often depicted as the human face facilitating the familiarization of the technological alien, presenting at the same time a human presence and a distance from it. (We might think also of the film E.T. as an early version of this.)

These child-machine analogies have frequently rendered individuals and collectives into things that can be adapted to dominant economic and political requirements (see Gordo López and Parker, 1999). In the nineteenth century with the rise of industrial culture in the West, the relationship between the human and the technological reached its apotheosis in the principles of scientific management of F. W. Taylor. As Sey (1999) indicates, the success of Taylorism in its aim to integrate the human body with industrial technology was to find its most famous realization in the new scientific management theory of Fordism. Like Taylorism, this sought to maximize the body-machine adjustment. Yet Fordism attempted to transcend the biological limits of the human body, a body whose irrational feelings and biological needs were considered limited and dysfunctional from the point of view of the emerging industrial concern with machine culture.

At the heart of this modernist technological endeavor, as Sey (1999, pp. 32–33) puts it, "was the attempt to improve productivity in labour contexts, but the attempt to isolate and decompose the body's extension and duration meant the technology began to manifest itself as an attempt to reduce distance and time to the condition of instantaneity and presence. . . . which extends its agency, to the erasure of the trace of the technology itself."

But the modern technologies (of reproduction) moved on to new cultural and "entertainment" dimensions, as illustrated by Benjamin (1973). The changing body-machine relation not only corresponded and adapted to different economic and industrial regimes. Beyond this, a huge rise in service technologies (such as cinema photography) and, more recently, information technologies has also involved the redrawing of emotional and biological boundaries, as we now move on to argue.

## Conclusion

Stepping back from our current technocultural condition entails gaining a wider understanding of the role of metaphors of childhood and discourses around children, as articulated within and mobilized by the mass media. It also means moving away from humanistic, psychologizing, and pedagogical concerns. These new discourses both incorporate and transcend longstanding binaries such as adult-child, reason-emotion, private-public, hardware-software, and inner-outer space. They go beyond the terrain of modern and postmodern analogies portraying childhood as the sphere of playfulness, incontinent desire, creativity, and transgression (Lyotard, 1992), which nevertheless retains modern inflections (Burman, 1998b).

Currently, a plethora of new processes are emerging in which technology is increasingly becoming a form of biology and where emotions, along with psychology, increasingly enter into notions of economy and government. Far from mere coincidence, managerial concern with emotional intelligence functions within a context where feelings and emotions are vital resources within the virtual and global economy. As de Kerckhove (1999, 2001) notes, emotions are a major part of the current electronic economy in which the most important economic events are exposed to what Robert McIllwraith (cited in de Kerckhove, 1999) described as the "feelings economy." For investment is based on feelings provoked by the rumor and the manipulation of economic optimism, anxiety, and caution (de Kerckhove, 1999). In short, as de Kerckhove puts it, "Economy is very susceptible to emotions and feelings" (p. 194).

All of these interrelated changes are taking place at once. Some authors gather them under the label of "connectivity," defined as the tendency to join and relate independent entities, without previous connections (de Kerckhove, 1999).

According to the connectivity thesis, inner and outer processes are being dislocated. The inner finds an external surface and mode of existence in the connected mass media, making a direct and collective connection between machines and human mind. This anticipates a shift from memory (knowledge, statistic, techniques of regulation: "learning machines") to more dynamic, self-regulated forms based on notions of intelligence, albeit of a highly emotional, biotechnological, and liquid and dematerialized kind (as with the electronic global economy).

The surfaces of resistance of human biology, and its capacity to be socially organized, now find new possibilities in the dance of the fluid ontology that seems to characterize the establishment of network society (Castells, 1996). At this moment, there is not only a suppression of previous fears associated with combining the body with technological devices (as in the coupling of tools, animals, humans, and unknown forces), but also an urgent synergy being formed between biology, technologies, and the self. When early twentieth-century industrial technology depicted human bodies behaving like machines, biology was seen as an obstacle to be adjusted to gain full output on the assembly line. The biological impediments foreseen by early scientific management are now less of a problem with the arrival of, for example, new childlike and highly emotional activities that are epitomized by the Teletubbies. Here we might note that underneath the hyperreal pastoral hillocks on which the Teletubbies frolic lies a much more technological and functional habitat.

The distance between technology and the body seems to have been reduced by means of devices that naturalize such distance with the aid of new biotechnological mediations and textures. In other words, the Teletubbies are immersed in our screen as much as the screen and child discourses are incorporated in their Teletummies/tubbies. These sorts of embodiments also enable us to reflect back further on our bodies and their place in our social imaginary.

We want to go further than Buckingham when he argues that children's television programs such as *Teletubbies* (and the advertising campaigns discussed here) blur the boundaries between the private and the public, the body and the technology, between childhood and adulthood. They also blur the boundaries between biology and technology, between psychology and technology, and between reason and emotion. In this integrating and redefining process, the processing of data and information technologies respectively move from the management of data to the connecting together—literally the plugging—of biological, technological, and social bodies.

This relation has its correspondence in more recent cultural texts as, for instance, Stephen Spielberg's adaptation of P. K. Dick's (1956, in 1991) short science fiction novel has recently shown. Released in 2002, this science fiction thriller, entitled *Minority Report,* takes place in some not-too-distant future in which human-like biology is already part of wider structures of information, prediction, and surveillance. Biology, combined with information technologies and the police apparatus, is able to predict inner criminal intentions and drives, and thanks to the high degree of connectivity, these links can be translated onto public screens and prompt action to counter these supposed inner desires for crime.

It is in the light of these processes that we can understand de Kerckhove's notion that during the past fifty years, leading to the invention of virtual reality, the virtualization and the convergence of sensorial values, textures, structures, and hardware properties, "the contents are not merely transforming *software* but in a more radical way, or *mindware*" (de Kerckhove, 1999, p. 174, our translation). What de Kerckhove understands by *mindware* is "a type of software based on the knowledge of mass media, that is, a kind of software closely connected to human processors, not merely mechanic ones" (p. 179). In this way, mindware is already at work in the film. The bio-information of bodies and their participation in networks of surveillance was supposedly able to detect unconscious desires, as well as reconstructing the flow of events in ways yet unknown by the social actors (or potential criminals) or not even accessible to or lived by them.

Such new configurations of mind and body through developments in the human-technology interface involve an inversion of traditional psychological terms that have traditionally portrayed a move from inner to outer screen-contact surfaces, and this inversion has been rendered possible by the mass media and, especially, ideological and surveillance apparatuses that punctuate and signify them. These levels of connectivity permit the re-creation and expansion of a world with amplified minds for education, work, play, love, and health. In this way, virtual reality is something other than a shared hallucination. Whether personally experienced or not, its very existence ushers in a new form of connected reality that offers enormous potential for the intensification of all sorts of regulation, mediation, and resignifying practices (Parker, 1997).

In this context, the unfixed and ungoverned metaphor of the child as produced under, and as an effect of, historically informed but currently shifting conditions emerges as a new privileged site for experimenting with the amplification of realities. This is due mainly to its flexibility and the capacity to project and adjust itself to the dimension of augmented reality. The developing child and other associated cultural metaphors advance the process of connectivity in the service of global and fluid market.

The child is also a rich surface on which to project the new psychological terms, and corresponding forms, of social and economic relations. The question to pose here, then, is how to specify what these changing self-organizing principles are doing. In what ways do the figures of the child and emotion emerge as new spaces for redefining and constructing forms of subjects working, as Foucault (1994) has suggested, as instruments of reason? To what extent do they offer surfaces that are already mediated and so emotionally compatible with newly emerging regimes, and to what extent does their particular configuration lend themselves to resistance? Either way, and notwithstanding the long-standing links between emotion, childhood, governmentality, and the market, it is clear that metaphors of the technochild and emotional capital have recently acquired a new centrality. The question of whether this simply recapitulates old themes (to which we might respond, unlike the Teletubbies, by saying, "Not again!") or offers some new rhetorical spaces for the elaboration of more enabling representations of agency remains unresolved.

## Notes

1. We are indebted to Angeles Díez, who kindly drew our attention to this mass media persuasion strategy, including that of "dead babies' histories," in the context of mass media participation in the justification and, most important, in the construction of recent imperialist Western warfare.

2. We are drawing here on the more extensive discussion of this marketing included in M. Ángeles González Lobo (2002).

## References

Álvarez-Uría, F. "'Retórica Neoliberal.'" In F. Álvarez-Uría and others (eds.), *Neoliberalismo vs Democracia*. Madrid: La Piqueta, 1998.

Aristotle. *Rhetoric*. In R. McKeon (ed.), *The Basic Works of Aristotle*. London: Random House, 1941.

Ashforth, B. E., and Humphrey, R. H. "Emotion in the Workplace: A Reappraisal." *Human Relations*, 1995, 48(2), 97–125.

Averill, J. R. "An Analysis of Psychophysiological Symbolism and Its Influence on Theories of Emotion." In R. Harré and W. Gerrod Parrot (eds.), *The Emotions: Social, Cultural and Biological Dimensions*. Thousand Oaks, Calif.: Sage, 1996.

Barglow, R. *The Crisis of the Self in the Age of Information*. New York: Routledge, 1994.

Benjamin, W. "The Work of Art in the Age of Mechanical Reproduction." In W. Benjamin, *Illuminations*. Augsburg Fortress, Minn.: Fontana Press, 1973.

Birke, L. *Women, Feminism and Biology*. Lewes: Harvester, 1982.

Boyatzis, R. "Los líderes que necesitamos hoy." *El País*, Jan. 25–26, 2003, p. 2.

Brockman, J. "The Emerging Third Culture." In J. Brockman (ed.), *The Third Culture: Beyond the Scientific Revolution*, New York: Simon & Schuster, 1995.

Brown, M. "Parents: A Spot of Tubby Trouble." *Guardian*, May, 21, 1997, p. 14.

Buckingham, D. "Blurring the Boundaries `Teletubbies' and Children's Media Today." *Televizion,* 1999, *12*(2), 8–12.

Burman, E. "The Abnormal Distribution of Development: Child Development and Policies for Southern Women." *Gender, Place and Culture,* 2(1), 21–36, 1995.

Burman, E. "The Child, the Woman and the Cyborg." In K. Henwood, C. Griffin and A. Phoenix (eds.), *Standpoints and Differences: Essays in the Practice of Feminist Psychology.* Thousand Oaks, Calif.: Sage, 1998a.

Burman, E. "Pedagogics of Post/Modernity: The Address to the Child in Walter Benjamin and Jean-François Lyotard." In K. Lesnik-Oberstein (ed.), *Children in Culture: Approaches to Childhood.* Old Tappan, N.J.: Macmillan, 1998b.

Burman, E. "Rhetorics of Psychological Development; From Complicity to Resistance." *Interacoes,* 1999a, *4*(8), 11–24.

Burman, E. "Appealing and Appalling Children." *Psychoanalytic Studies,* 1999b, *1*(3), 285–302.

Burman, E. "Beyond the Baby and the Bathwater: Post-Dualist Developmental Psychology." *European Early Childhood Education Research Journal,* 2001, *9*(1), 5–22.

Burman, E. "Children and Sexuality: Contested Relationships Around the Control of Desire and Activity." Paper presented at the Contested Childhood Seminar Program, Advanced Study Centre, International Institute, University of Michigan, Ann Arbor, Apr. 2002.

Burman, E. "Childhood and Contemporary Political Subjectivities." In S. Warner and P. Reavey (eds.), *Challenging the Tyranny of Truth: New Feminist Stories of Child Sexual Abuse.* New York: Routledge, 2003.

Castells, M. *The Information Age: Economy, Society and Culture,* Vol. 1: *The Rise of the Network Society.* Cambridge, Mass.: Blackwell, 1996.

Daly, S., and Wice, N. *Alt. Culture: An A-Z of the 90s, Underground and Online.* London: Fourth Estate/Guardian Books, 1995.

de Kerckhove D. *Inteligencias en conexión. Hacia una sociedad de la web.* Barcelona: Gedisa, 1999.

de Kerckhove, D. "End of the Beginning for the Internet." [http://mondediplo.com/2001/08/10internet]. 2001.

Dick, P. K. *The Minority Report-The Collected Short Stories of P. K. Dick,* Vol. 4. New York: Citadel Press, 1956/1991.

Elster, J. *Alchemies of the Mind.* Cambridge: Cambridge University Press, 1999.

Foucault, M. *The Order of Things.* New York: Vintage, 1994.

Giddens, A. *The Transformation of Intimacy: Sexuality, Love and Eroticism in Modern Societies.* Cambridge: Polity Press, 1992.

Giddens, A. *Runaway World: How Globalization Is Reshaping Our Lives.* New York: Routledge, 2000.

Goleman, D. *Emotional Intelligence.* New York: Bantam Books, 1995.

Goleman, D., Boyatzis, R., and McKee, A. *Primal Leadership: Realizing the Power of Emotional Intelligence.* Boston: Harvard Business School Press, 2002.

Gordo López, A. J. "Amores On-line/Off-line." *Teknokultura,* 2001. [http://tekno kultura.rrp.upr.edu/teknosphera/amores_on_line.htm].

Gordo López, A. J. "Función de las Nuevas Tecnologías en la Construcción de la Identidad: Una mirada cualitativa desde la Emoción y el Tacto." In A. Baustista García-Vera (ed.), *Las nuevas tecnologías y su utilización pedagógica en la escuela.* Madrid: Akal, 2003.

Gordo López, A. J., and Parker, I. "Cyberpsychology: Postdisciplinary Contexts and Projects." In A. J. Gordo López and I. Parker (eds.), *Cyberpsychology.* Old Tappan, N.J.: Macmillan, 1999.

Greenberg, M. T., Kusche, C. A., Cook, E. T., and Quamma, J. P. "Promoting Emotional Competence in School-Aged Children: The Effects of the PATHS Curriculum." *Development and Psychopathology,* 1995, *7*, 117–136.

Haraway, D. *Primate Vision: Gender, Race and Nature in the World of Modern Science.* New York: Routledge, 1989.

Harré, R. *The Social Construction of Emotions.* Cambridge, Mass.: Basil Blackwell, 1986.

Howard, S., and Roberts, S. "'Teletubbies' Down Under: The Australian Experience." *Televizion,* 1999, *12*(2), 19–25.

Huhtamo, E. "From Cybernation to Interaction. A Contribution to an Archaeology of Interactivity." In C. Giannetti (ed.), *Marcel-lí Antúnez Roca.* Madrid: Fundación Telefónica, 1999.

Lutz, C. A. "Engendered Emotion: Gender, Power, and the Rhetoric of Emotion Control in American Discourse." In R. Harré and W. Gerrod Parrot (eds.), *The Emotions: Social, Cultural and Biological Dimensions.* Thousand Oaks, Calif.: Sage, 1996.

Lutz, C. A., and White, G. A. "The Anthropology of Emotions." *Annual Review of Anthropology,* 1986, *15,* 405–36.

Lyotard, J. *The Postmodern Explained to Children: Correspondence, 1982–1985.* London: Turnaround, 1992.

Mainstream Media. "Guerra, propaganda y los medios de comunicación." *Rebelión,* Oct. 25, 2001. [http://www.globalissues.org/HumanRights/Media/Military.asp?Print=True].

Marinas, J. A. *El laberinto sentimental.* Barcelona: Anagrama, 1996.

Mayer, J. D., and Salovey, P. "The Intelligence of Emotional Intelligence." *Intelligence,* 1993, *17,* 433–442.

Movistar. "E-moción." [http://www.movistar.com/empresas/servicios/emocion/emocion2.htm]. 2001.

Parker, I. *Psychoanalytic Culture: Psychoanalytic Discourse in Western Society.* Thousand Oaks, Calif.: Sage, 1997.

Parkinson, B. *Ideas and Realities of Emotion.* New York: Routledge, 1995.

Reeve, C.D.C. "Aristotle's Ethics." [http://batesca.tripod.com/Reevesethics.htm]. 2002.

Robinson, D. N. "Aristotle on the Emotions." In R. Harré and W. Gerrod Parrot (eds.), *The Emotions: Social, Cultural and Biological Dimensions.* Thousand Oaks, Calif.: Sage, 1996.

Rose, N. *Inventing Ourselves.* New York: Routledge, 1996.

Schäfer, A. "It Won't Work Without Breaking Taboos." *Televizion,* 1999, *12*(2), 5–7.

Sey, J. "The Labouring Body and the Posthuman." In A. J. Gordo-López and I. Parker (eds.), *Cyberpsychology.* Old Tappan, N.J.: Macmillan, 1999.

Steedman, C. "Strange Dislocations: Childhood and Sense of Human Interiority." *Gender and Society,* 1995, *1*(1), 85–109.

Svaóek, M. "The Politics of Emotions. Emotional Discourses and Displays in Post–Cold War Context." *Focaal European Journal of Anthropology,* 2002, *39,* 9–27. [http://www.focaal.box.nl/previous/ intro_39.pdf].

Thorndike, E. L. "Intelligence and Its Uses." *Harper's Magazine,* 1920, *140,* 227–235.

Walkerdine, V. *The Mastery of Reason: Cognitive Development and the Production of Rationality.* New York: Routledge, 1988.

White, A. M. "To Be Blamed: The Press in Britain." *Televizion,* 1999, *12*(2), 15–18.

ÁNGEL J. GORDO LÓPEZ *is a lecturer in sociology at the Universidad Complutense de Madrid.*

ERICA BURMAN *is professor of psychology and women's studies at Manchester Metropolitan University, U.K., where she codirects the Discourse Unit and the Women's Studies Research Centre.*

# INDEX

Tapscott, D., 3, 14
Telecommunication technologies: broad-band, 29–32; cross-cultural dimension of, 26–27; text-based, 26
*Teletubbies* (children's television program), national debate over, 71–73, 76
Thomas, B., 6
Thorndike, E. L., 65
Toffler, A., 17
Turkle, S., 16, 26, 41, 44

U.S. Education Department's National Center for Educational Statistics, 12
U.S. Federal Trade Commission, 44

van Duuren, M. A., 43
Venezky, R. L., 43
Vgotsky, L. S., 42, 46, 51
Video games, and child behavior, 35
Virtual reality systems, 26

Walkerdine, V., 64
Wallace, P., 16
Wang, F. M., 43
Ware, N., 8
Web mail service, international distribution of, 15

Weil, M. M., 44, 51, 52
Wenger, D., 19
Werner, H., 46
Westerink, J.H.D.M., 44
Westerman, S. J., 43
White, A. M., 71, 72
White, G. A., 64
Whitely, B., 52
Wice, N., 72
Williams, R. L., 51
Williams, Ś., 52
Williamson, P. A., 43
Woodburn, W., 52
Wright, J. C., 42, 55

Xu, W., 43

Yan, Z., 46, 50
Young, K. S., 44
Yuan, Y., 43
Yumiko, H., 34
Yumiko, T., 34

Zakon, H., 4
Zammit, K., 44
Zizi, M., 43
Zohar, A., 46

# Back Issue/Subscription Order Form

Copy or detach and send to:

**Jossey-Bass, A Wiley Company, 989 Market Street, San Francisco CA 94103-1741**

**Call or fax toll-free: Phone 888-378-2537 6:30AM – 3PM PST; Fax 888-481-2665**

Back Issues:     Please send me the following issues at $29 each
(Important: please include series initials and issue number, such as CAD96.)

_____

_____

_____

$ _____   Total for single issues

$ _____   SHIPPING CHARGES:  SURFACE     Domestic        Canadian
First Item      $5.00           $6.00
Each Add'l Item   $3.00         $1.50
For next-day and second-day delivery rates, call the number listed above.

Subscriptions:     Please __start __renew my subscription to *New Directions for Child and Adolescent Development* for the year 2_____ at the following rate:

| | | |
|---|---|---|
| U.S. | __Individual $90 | __Institutional $205 |
| Canada | __Individual $90 | __Institutional $245 |
| All Others | __Individual $114 | __Institutional $279 |
| U.S. Online Subscription | | __Institutional $205 |
| U.S. Print and Online Subscription | | __Institutional $226 |

**For more information about online subscriptions visit
www.interscience.wiley.com**

$_____   Total single issues and subscriptions (Add appropriate sales tax for your state for single issue orders. No sales tax for U.S. subscriptions. Canadian residents, add GST for subscriptions and single issues.)

__Payment enclosed (U.S. check or money order only)
__VISA __MC __AmEx #_____ Exp. Date _____

Signature _____ Day Phone _____
__ Bill Me (U.S. institutional orders only. Purchase order required.)

Purchase order # _____
**Federal Tax ID13559302**                    **GST 89102 8052**

Name _____

Address _____

_____

Phone _____ E-mail _____

For more information about Jossey-Bass, visit our Web site at **www.josseybass.com**

## NEW DIRECTIONS FOR
## CHILD AND ADOLESCENT DEVELOPMENT
## IS NOW AVAILABLE ONLINE AT WILEY INTERSCIENCE

## What is Wiley InterScience?

*Wiley InterScience* is the dynamic online content service from John Wiley & Sons delivering the full text of over 300 leading scientific, technical, medical, and professional journals, plus major reference works, the acclaimed Current Protocols laboratory manuals, and even the full text of select Wiley print books online.

## What are some special features of Wiley InterScience?

*Wiley Interscience Alerts* is a service that delivers table of contents via e-mail for any journal available on Wiley InterScience as soon as a new issue is published online.
*EarlyView* is Wiley's exclusive service presenting individual articles online as soon as they are ready, even before the release of the compiled print issue. These articles are complete, peer-reviewed, and citable.
*CrossRef* is the innovative multi-publisher reference linking system enabling readers to move seamlessly from a reference in a journal article to the cited publication, typically located on a different server and published by a different publisher.

## How can I access Wiley InterScience?

Visit http://www.interscience.wiley.com.

*Guest Users* can browse Wiley InterScience for unrestricted access to journal tables of contents and article abstracts, or use the powerful search engine.
*Registered Users* are provided with a *Personal Home Page* to store and manage customized alerts, searches, and links to favorite journals and articles. Additionally, Registered Users can view free online sample issues and preview selected material from major reference works.
*Licensed Customers* are entitled to access full-text journal articles in PDF, with select journals also offering full-text HTML.

## How do I become an Authorized User?

*Authorized Users* are individuals authorized by a paying Customer to have access to the journals in Wiley InterScience. For example, a university that subscribes to Wiley journals is considered to be the Customer. Faculty, staff and students authorized by the university to have access to those journals in Wiley InterScience are Authorized Users. Users should contact their library for information on which Wiley journals they have access to in Wiley InterScience.

## ASK YOUR INSTITUTION ABOUT WILEY INTERSCIENCE TODAY!